Alan Titchmarsh
how to garden

Lawns, Paths and Patios

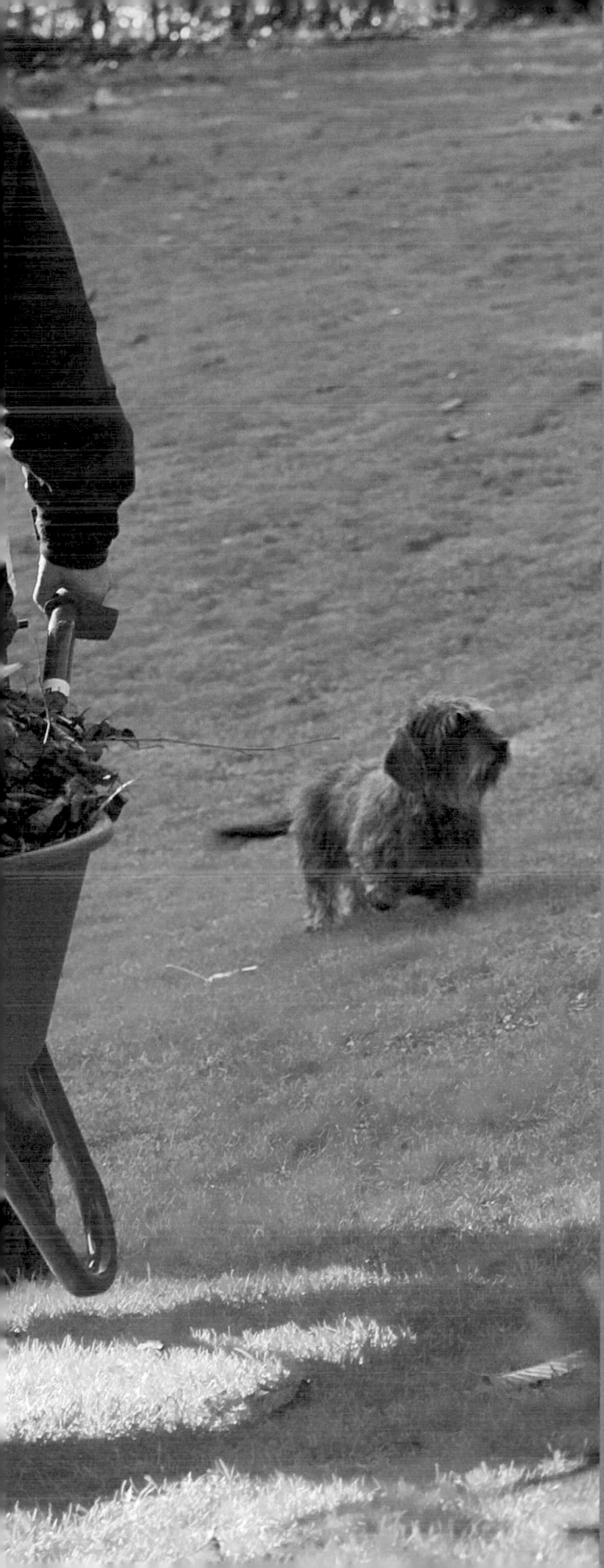

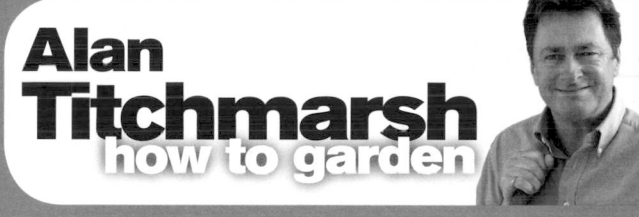

Alan Titchmarsh

how to garden

Lawns, Paths and Patios

BBC BOOKS

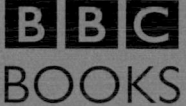

10 9 8 7 6 5 4 3 2 1

Published in 2009 by BBC Books, an imprint of
Ebury Publishing, a Random House Group Company

The Random House Group Limited Reg. No. 954009

Addresses for companies within the Random House
Group can be found at
www.randomhouse.co.uk

The Random House Group Limited supports The Forest
Stewardship Council (FSC), the leading international
forest certification organisation. All our titles that are
printed on Greenpeace approved FSC certified paper
carry the FSC logo. Our paper procurement policy can be
found at www.rbooks.co.uk/environment

A CIP catalogue record for this book is available from
the British Library.

ISBN 978 1 84 6073984

Produced by Outhouse!
Shalbourne, Marlborough, Wiltshire SN8 3QJ

BBC BOOKS
COMMISSIONING EDITORS: Lorna Russell, Stuart Cooper
PROJECT EDITOR: Caroline McArthur
PRODUCTION CONTROLLER: Phil Spencer

OUTHOUSE!
CONCEPT DEVELOPMENT & PROJECT MANAGEMENT:
   Elizabeth Mallard-Shaw
CONTRIBUTING EDITOR: Jo Weeks
PROJECT EDITOR: Polly Boyd
ART DIRECTION: Robin Whitecross
SERIES DESIGN: Sharon Cluett
DESIGNER: Robin Whitecross
ILLUSTRATOR: Lizzie Harper

PHOTOGRAPHS by Jonathan Buckley except where
credited otherwise on page 128

Colour origination by Altaimage, London
Printed and bound by Firmengruppe APPL,
Wemdig, Germany

Contents

Introduction

Gardening is one of the best and most fulfilling activities on earth, but it can sometimes seem complicated and confusing. The answers to problems can usually be found in books, but big fat gardening books can be rather daunting. Where do you start? How can you find just the information you want without wading through lots of stuff that is not appropriate to your particular problem? Well, a good index is helpful, but sometimes a smaller book devoted to one particular subject fits the bill better – especially if it is reasonably priced and if you have a small garden where you might not be able to fit in everything suggested in a larger volume.

The *How to Garden* books aim to fill that gap – even if sometimes it may be only a small one. They are clearly set out and written, I hope, in a straightforward, easy-to-understand style. I don't see any point in making gardening complicated, when much of it is based on common sense and observation. (All the key techniques are explained and illustrated, and I've included plenty of tips and tricks of the trade.)

There are suggestions on the best plants and the best varieties to grow in particular situations and for a particular effect. I've tried to keep the information crisp and to the point so that you can find what you need quickly and easily and then put your new-found knowledge into practice. Don't worry if you're not familiar with

the Latin names of plants. They are there to make sure you can find the plant as it will be labelled in the nursery or garden centre, but where appropriate I have included common names, too. Forgetting a plant's name need not stand in your way when it comes to being able to grow it.

Above all, the *How to Garden* books are designed to fill you with passion and enthusiasm for your garden and all that its creation and care entails, from designing and planting it to maintaining it and enjoying it. For more than fifty years gardening has been my passion, and that initial enthusiasm for watching plants grow, for trying something new and for just being outside pottering has never faded. If anything I am keener on gardening now than I ever was and get more satisfaction from my plants every day. It's not that I am simply a romantic, but rather that I have learned to look for the good in gardens and in plants, and there is lots to be found. Oh, there are times when I fail – when my plants don't grow as well as they should and I need to try harder. But where would I rather be on a sunny day? Nowhere!

The *How to Garden* handbooks will, I hope, allow some of that enthusiasm – childish though it may be – to rub off on you, and the information they contain will, I hope, make you a better gardener, as well as opening your eyes to the magic of plants and flowers.

Introducing lawns and hard surfaces

Ask any child, or adult for that matter, to make a quick sketch of a house and they'll inevitably draw a square building with a path leading to the front door and lawn on either side. It's our idealized view of home – a welcoming place where we feel secure, and a garden is an integral part of this ideal. But it's not just about plants, it's also about having an outdoor living area where children can play and adults can relax. In most gardens about two-thirds of the space consists of lawns and hard surfaces, so it's important they look good and are of practical use. Artists paint a picture and then choose a suitable frame. Garden design differs in that the 'frame', or hard landscaping, needs to be made first and then the picture 'painted' with plants.

Choosing a surface

Lawns, paths, patios, terraces and decks are the flat surfaces that make up our garden, or link its various parts. While lawns and paths are easily defined, the distinction between patios, terraces and decks is blurred, and in practice they often perform similar duties. The design and the materials that go into the construction of garden surfaces are determined by their situation as well as your personal preferences and budget. Consider the visual effect you want to achieve and always balance it with the practicalities.

If you're planning a new lawn or area of hard surfacing, begin by thinking about how you'll use the space – for example, a patio for entertaining is quite different from a utilitarian place where you hang the washing or keep the bins, and the aesthetic, practical and financial decisions you make should reflect this. Also, bear in mind the amount of work involved, both in the area's construction and its long-term upkeep. Try to be realistic in your aims: it's no good hankering after a lush green sward if you're a couch potato, because it will require too much aftercare. Likewise, there's no point in establishing a super-fine lawn if the kids play football on the grass – it simply won't withstand the wear. Consider that your needs are likely to change over time and plan for any adaptations you may want to make later on.

This informal stepped path (above) is understated and rustic, with plants left to creep naturally among the cobbles. In contrast, a groomed lawn (below) is striking and stately.

Lawns

The lawn is so much more than just an expanse of grass to be looked at and admired. It's marvellously refreshing to relax on or beside the lawn on a warm day, gazing up at the blue sky and watching birds and insects going about their daily lives. And a lawn is wonderful for the senses – rich green seems to have a calming effect, and at the height of summer, there's nothing quite like walking barefoot on freshly mown grass for making you feel good.

A lawn is easily adapted according to your needs, your budget and the time you're willing or able to devote to its upkeep. If you want an immaculate, carefully manicured area, complete with parallel stripes, you'll need a fine grass mixture and plenty of time at your disposal. If, on the other hand, you have children who want to play on the grass, you'll require a lawn that can pretty much take care of itself. Inevitably, if it gets plenty of use it will become worn in some areas and need restorative care at the end of the summer, but grass is a resilient plant and by choosing a hardwearing mixture you should be able to have a lawn that can stand a reasonable amount of wear and tear without too much long-term suffering. Mine does!

You can create a lawn on any garden soil, either by sowing seed or laying turf. Whatever you choose, a lawn needs a minimum level of attention without which it will struggle. Care

This circular lawn, surrounded by an edging of bricks, makes the perfect calm companion to the mixed shrubby planting around it.

Take time out to relax and enjoy your lawn after a long, hard day. It's incredibly soothing and therapeutic.

Lawns: the pros and cons

- Grass is an evergreen, resilient, natural landscaping material.
- Lawns fit in with any garden design.
- The plain green colour of a lawn links different garden elements together and acts as a cool, soothing foil to the brighter flower colours.
- A lawn creates a sense of calm openness that is a perfect complement to the planted areas, which might otherwise seem quite full and busy.
- Turf is easy to lay.
- The shape and make up of a lawn can be tailored to suit the area to be covered and its usage.
- Freshly mown grass feels good underfoot and smells lovely.
- Grass releases oxygen, so it's good for the environment. It's also wildlife friendly.

BUT...

- A fair amount of hard work is needed to keep it looking good.
- Sunshine and good drainage are both required, so you need to ensure the site is suitable (*see* pages 30–1, 33–4).
- Lawns need mowing at least once and sometimes twice a week, apart from in the depths of winter, and regular edging.
- A lawn will turn brown and straw-like in prolonged dry weather and needs spring and autumn feeds to keep it healthy and green.
- To remove the build-up of thatch a lawn needs annual scarifying.
- You may have to treat a lawn for moss, weeds, and pests and diseases.
- A lawn may need restorative work where it receives heavy use.

Pots of ornamental topiary flank the stone steps that lead to a perfect lawn complete with stripes – the centrepiece of this formal garden.

Grass makes a great playing surface for kids. It might suffer within this willow playhouse in summer, but can recover during the winter months.

includes regular mowing, occasional raking and spiking, and an annual or twice-yearly feeding and weeding session. If you're not prepared to do this amount of work, it makes good sense to consider an alternative to grass. You also need to work out the logistics of cutting the grass (whether you can get a mower onto the area) and the conditions it will be growing in (especially the type of soil, *see* pages 32–3).

Flanked by vibrant flowers and foliage, this stone path provides a breathing space in a lush garden, as well as leading you to a welcome seating area.

Paths have an important part to play in the overall look of the garden. Here, a gravel path sets off to perfection this collection of drought-tolerant plants.

Paths

Just like lawns, paths vary according to their position and use. If a path simply links one place to another, such as the house to the garage, it can be straight and functional. If, however, it's intended to lead the eye into the garden and encourage you to enter and explore the space, it plays a large part in the design of the garden as a whole. Depending on your overall plan for the garden, it could still be straight, leading you directly to one spot, or it could meander and become a point of interest in itself. The materials that are used to create a path should reflect its purpose.

Concrete, paving stones, bricks, gravel and bark chippings, or a combination of these, are all commonly used to make paths, and all produce a different result (*see* page 70). For a heavily used path

In a wildflower meadow, mown grass paths are the best choice. These complement the natural look and can be created as and when they're needed.

Stepping stones keep most foot traffic off the grass on this narrow strip of lawn, which would otherwise be subject to wear. They also tempt you to walk on down through the garden to find out what's there.

that leads to the utility area of a garden, such as the dustbins or washing line, a hardwearing material is most suitable, whereas a path that winds through a shrub border is more for decoration than day-to-day use and might be more attractive surfaced with bark chippings. Depending on what they're made from, paths can be high maintenance (gravel) or low maintenance (concrete or paving).

Underlining the transition from a formal garden to a more relaxed area, this path cleverly changes from neatly laid pebbles enclosed by brick edging to chunky natural stone.

Geometric shapes and crisp lines predominate in this garden and are matched by the smooth slate patio surface. The pale wooden loungers highlight the limited colour palette.

A sheltered patio makes a wonderful dining area and the wooden pergola above offers plenty of opportunities for planting ornamental climbers.

Patios

The word 'patio' was originally used to describe an inner courtyard, surrounded by the living quarters of a building. Today, it is used more generally to refer to an outdoor seating area that is usually attached to the back or side of a house and is frequently paved.

Patios are a very popular way to extend the living space into the garden. Most are built with the idea of providing an alfresco dining area and so should be large enough to fit a table and chairs with ease. They can be very simple or more complex, with walls, raised planters, steps and other decorative details. The most popular material for patios is paving, because it's versatile, flat and long lasting, but other materials, including brick, wood or gravel, are perfectly acceptable, depending on the effect you want to achieve (*see* page 70).

The most convenient place to build a patio is beside the house. This allows for easy access from the kitchen and other rooms, and encourages you to use the patio on every suitable occasion. However, it's important to take into account shelter, privacy, sun and shade when deciding on its position. It's no good having a beautiful patio that's in the shade from four o'clock in the afternoon and receives the full blast of all the cold winds. While you can create some form of screening to reduce the effects of wind, you will feel the lack of sun on all but the very hottest of days.

Patios: the pros and cons

- A patio provides additional space for rest, relaxation and entertaining.

- A seating area near the house gives you a vantage point from which to enjoy the rest of the garden.

- Patios dry off quickly after rain, meaning you can go outside without getting wet or muddy, or damaging the grass.

- A paved area can provide the ideal place for a small child to play on a warm day, under the watchful eye of a parent near by.

- A patio can form part of the overall design of the garden, providing structure and form, especially through the winter.

BUT...

- The better-quality or more unusual paving materials can be expensive.

- Paving must be properly laid with a fall to allow drainage and a good foundation (*see* pages 72–4). If you don't do this yourself, it can be costly.

- Seating areas need careful siting to avoid too much sun/shade/overlooking.

- A patio will need cleaning, sweeping, and possibly weeding and moss and algae treatment.

- Paving may deteriorate, especially if it has been badly laid. It can also become unstable and uneven, eventually creating a trip hazard.

- Inexpensive, poor-quality materials will discolour over time.

- Unless it's on the level, a patio will need railings or some sort of barrier as a safety measure.

This inviting terrace, looking down over the water, contains a variety of materials but their use is subtle, which avoids a busy or distracting result.

Terraces

A terrace can be a level area created on a hillside, a raised seating area, a patio on a rooftop or even a large balcony. The word has many connotations, but in a garden situation it usually refers to a raised, flat seating area: a patio that sits at the top of a sloping garden could easily be called a terrace.

Like a patio, a terrace can be constructed from a range of materials depending on its situation and use. Privacy, shelter and comfort are also equally important on a terrace. If, however, the terrace is an integral part of the house – for example, if it's built above some ground-floor rooms – its design will be dictated by building constraints.

A generous-sized terrace forms a useful bridge between two garden levels.

Roof gardens

A roof garden is a definite plus in a crowded city or town, but it can be created anywhere and provides a uniquely private and secluded space. Even so, there are some very important practical considerations that must be taken into account before building one, as the last thing you want is for the roof to tumble into the sitting room or the water that you're giving your plants to find

Wood, metal and large architectural plants link the two levels of this contemporary two-storeyed roof terrace, which also manages to be in keeping with the old-fashioned soft yellow of the London brick walls.

its way into the neighbour's house. It makes sense to have a structural engineer assess the space to ensure it's safe and have it designed and built by a professional who has had experience of such projects.

Decking

A deck is basically a patio or terrace made from wood. In countries where wood is readily available, it has always been a popular material for using in the garden. For example, wooden verandas are traditional and commonplace in Australia and many parts of the United States, where they complement the wooden houses to which they are attached. Decking is an extension

A secluded spot in the garden is the ideal site for a deck. Making good use of a small area, this one even has a built-in pond and walkway.

This combination of decking steps and landings offers the ideal solution for a big drop between house and garden.

of this idea and is particularly suited to waterside houses or homes that have a garden that slopes away from the house.

In recent years, 'decking' has come to refer to a particular type of surface built from narrowish planks that have longitudinal ridges cut into them. This is usually surrounded by a banister arrangement of some sort and supported on strong beams and uprights. However, a deck can

be made from any sort of wood and it can be arranged in a variety of ways (*see* pages 91–7). It's extremely versatile and is a wonderful way of creating a level seating area on any patch of land, no matter how uneven. It can be built against a building to give access over a low area without resorting to steps, and may have several levels to provide extra interest and make the space appear larger (*see* right and page 69).

Designing and planning

Creating a new area of lawn or hard landscaping can seem like a daunting task, particularly when it involves reorganizing other elements in the garden, as is often the case. First, familiarize yourself with the space, do some research into design and practical issues and then do a few sketches and scale drawings – a systematic approach will really help to focus the mind.

Assess your garden

Whether you're just putting in a new patio in an established garden or are designing a whole new garden from scratch, it's a great deal easier if you begin with a definite plan. You need to start by making an assessment of the plot. Get a large piece of paper and make a rough sketch of your house and garden. Include as much information as possible, such as where windows look onto the garden and the position of doors and other access points. Once you've made your basic drawing, the next job is to identify some of your garden's fixed characteristics, such as where it's sunny and shady, windy or sheltered, and any sloping areas that you need to take into account.

Aspect and exposure

Aspect is the direction in which the garden faces – north, south, east or west, or anywhere in between. It's crucial to be aware of a garden's aspect because it's fixed and affects everything in the garden. For example, the north side of your house will always be shadier than the south side, and in winter – when the sun stays fairly low in the sky all day – it will be even shadier than it is in summer. Most rain and wind will come from the south west, so that side of your house or garden will be more likely to need shelter in the form of a fence, hedge or a selection of tall, sturdy shrubs than the north-east side. However, don't forget that the winds that come from the north and east can be very cold.

To find out the aspect, get a directional compass or watch the sun as it passes over from dawn to dusk. Mark the sunny and shady areas on your sketch. Once you know this, you can work out where it makes sense to site the seating areas and the lawn – remember, grass doesn't thrive in heavily shaded situations. Also, wander outside on a windy day, and on

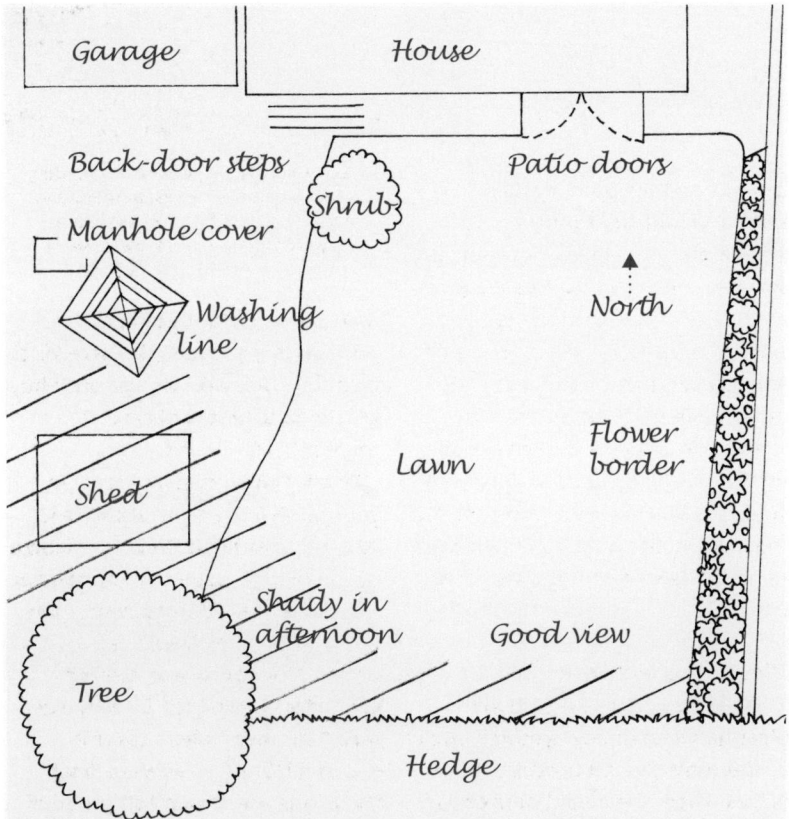

Labels on sketch: Garage · House · Back-door steps · Patio doors · Shrub · Manhole cover · Washing line · North · Shed · Lawn · Flower border · Shady in afternoon · Good view · Tree · Hedge

Don't forget

Before deciding on the position of a patio or seating area, think about when you'll use it most. For instance, if it's in the evening, look for the place that gets the most evening sun. Don't simply put it next to the house because it's convenient.

By making a detailed sketch of your garden you'll begin to become better acquainted with it. It's interesting to discover the spatial relationships between the various elements.

a rainy one, and find the most exposed parts of the garden and those that are more sheltered. Mark the areas on your sketch, noting where a screen or two would help to decrease the effects of wind and rain.

Topography

This is just a smart way of saying what the lie of the land is like. A garden that undulates or has low and high bits is more interesting than a completely flat one, but it can throw up design challenges.

If your garden slopes, you'll have to decide whether to work with the slope or to reduce it in some way. Usually, it's easier, and cheaper, to work with it. Ideally, a lawn will be on the flat, but a very gentle slope is also acceptable. A lawn on uneven

ground or a steep slope will be extremely difficult to mow. If you want a patio or other completely flat surface, you'll need to create a level area, or perhaps use decking. A slope can be lessened by terracing and retaining walls (*see* page 84), but it's a big job and you'll most likely need to factor in mechanical assistance. Can you get a digger into your garden? If not, be prepared to think again. Measure and mark any sloping areas on your drawing (*see* page 23).

Views and eyesores

Make a note of any particularly pleasing views or any eyesores, such as the compost and dustbins. Mark places where the neighbours can see into your garden and those that are

As the sun moves around the garden, some areas may be cast in shade for part of the day. Sun and shade also vary according to the season.

completely private. Using this information, you can plan screens or plantings that will disguise unsightly areas and draw attention to the more attractive parts.

If you have a manhole cover in your garden, try to incorporate it into a border rather than the middle of the lawn. If there is no option but for it to be centre stage, when you come to level the lawn site in preparation for sowing seed or laying turf (*see* pages 37–8) make sure that the manhole cover is 4–5cm (1½–2in) below the final level. This way it won't sit proud of the surface when the soil has settled.

Design considerations

If you're naturally artistic, or have been thinking about your new garden for a long while, you may well be ready to get down to the nitty gritty of the design process straight away. If, however, you need a bit of assistance, it may help you to know that professional garden designers like to take into account certain tried and tested design principles that have been about for centuries. Many of the design ideas given here are closely related, but it's easier to consider them separately at first.

Unity and integrity

Limit your choice of materials to two or three (or even fewer). Don't have a wooden deck, a brick path, a paved patio and a gravel drive. If you must have lots of different materials, link them by using shades of one colour – for instance, grey slate paving, blue-grey stained decking and grey slate chippings – or use complementary colours. If you want to introduce contrast, have one contrasting element or colour, rather than many.

Also, it's usually a good idea to select materials that complement the style of your house and surrounding buildings – is your house made of stone or brick, or is it rendered? What colours are the building materials? What is the period of the house? The materials you use don't need to match exactly or be historically accurate, but they should try to capture or enhance the general style and feel of the surrounding buildings if possible.

Balance and contrast

One of the most important ideas in garden design is to have unequal proportions of hard and soft landscaping. Don't, for example, make your garden half lawn and half

Straight lines and simple materials along with a limited range of colours have produced a peaceful but lush garden. The water adds a soothing element and reflects the landscape and sky.

There's plenty of energy in this sheltered corner, while the balance between hard and soft landscaping ensures the overall effect is pleasing. Diagonal lines in the paving, bench and fence create a strong sense of structure.

patio. Aim to have about one-quarter to one-third of your garden as hard landscaping (unless your garden is tiny and you want to pave the lot). You also need to aim to keep all the main features in proportion with one another, so nothing will dominate. Remember, it's better to have fewer, larger elements than many smaller ones – even in a small garden, this will create a sense of space.

All well-designed gardens contain contrasting elements to provide interest. If you have a busy area in the garden, such as a patio with plenty of detailing, balance this with a calm area, such as a sweep of lawn or a path with a plain surface. Counterbalance a flat, level lawn with shrubs in borders or a pergola covered with climbers.

It's easy to spot the drama queen in this carefully planted border – the large, spiky phormium is flanked by an array of other major and minor players, while the lawn throws the planting into relief.

A balance of vertical and horizontal dimensions is vital to provide interest. Combine low-growing plants with taller types, those with an upright habit with those that creep and sprawl. Choose some evergreen plants and some deciduous ones, so that you have something to look at all year round. Plant up some decorative containers to reduce the starkness of paving or decking (*see* pages 113–16).

Space and enclosure

It's amazing the effect that open spaces such as lawns and expanses of hard surfacing can have. Think about the contrasting emotions you feel when you look at a modern housing estate with all the front lawns linking into each other, and a traditional terraced row, where each house has its own walled or hedged front garden. The former provides a feeling of space where there may be none, while the latter gives a feeling of security, privacy and ownership. Create a sense of space and expansiveness with a lawn, patio or wide path that leads to a wonderful view; alternatively, if you want a feeling of enclosure, use a hedge, tree, screen or pergola. The rule of thumb is to balance these two elements in a proportion of approximately one to three (three parts open space to about one part enclosure).

Simple trellis fencing and an archway divide this garden, which is lushly planted on one side and more open on the other.

Creating the design

Now you should be fully armed with the information you need to come up with your own design. A good garden design looks effortless when completed – a harmony of plants and hard landscaping. But how do you go about achieving this yourself? Well, don't panic, it doesn't have to be difficult and you don't have to create an award-winning result. The most important thing is that you produce something you like and that you'll be able to maintain in the longer term.

Make a scale drawing

If you're planning a complete redesign, it's well worth measuring your garden accurately and making a scale drawing at this stage, using your rough sketch as a starting point. A scale drawing prevents all sorts of mistakes, such as having a patio that's too small or a shed that's too large. Even if you only want to add a patio or reshape the lawn, a decent drawing based on measurements taken using a long tape measure is a good place to start. Choose a permanent, straight fixed line as the baseline for taking the measurements – the wall of the house will do – and from there measure the distance to other fixed points, such as the corner of the garage, the corners of the garden, a tree, the clothes line and so on.

You'll find graph paper or maths-book-type paper makes your life easier – choose an easily workable scale, such as two squares to a metre. Mark on all the elements that you like and leave out those that you plan to get rid of. Take a few photocopies of this drawing so you can scribble on them as you come up with ideas and work out what should go where. This is all that any garden designer does. They do have the benefit of training and experience, and hopefully a naturally artistic eye, but you'll be surprised at what you can come up with if you experiment a little – after all, you organized the furniture in your sitting room, didn't you? Well, this is the same sort of idea, only it helps to draw it out first.

Recording a few measurements of fixed elements in the garden is one of the first steps to a successful design.

How to measure a slope

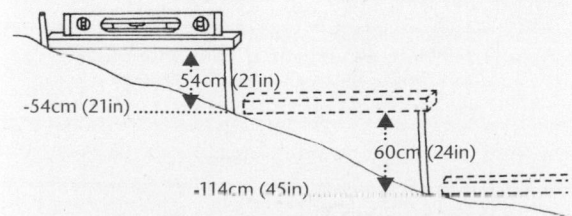

-54cm (21in)
54cm (21in)
60cm (24in)
-114cm (45in)

To measure the gradient of a slope, you'll need a spirit level, a narrow plank (about 1m/40in long) and a few pegs (lengths of 25mm/1in square battening). Before you start, draw a rough sketch of the slope.

① Insert a peg to mark the top of the slope and lay the plank beside the base of the peg, facing downhill.

② Just short of the lower end of the plank, drive a peg into the ground until its top is about level with the top of the slope. Balance the plank on top of the peg.

③ Put the spirit level on top of the plank and adjust the peg's height until the spirit level reads true level.

④ Measure the height of the plank from the ground. Record this figure on your sketch.

⑤ Working from the second peg, repeat the process described in steps 1–4 until you reach the bottom of the slope.

⑥ Add all the individual figures together to give you the overall drop of the slope and record the details on your sketch.

Adding new elements

This is the exciting bit. You'll probably find that after all the time you've spent measuring and sketching, ideas on how you'd like the garden to look will have been flitting in and out of your head, and hopefully you will have written some of them down. Keep the design simple, and don't go for anything fancy or wildly extravagant – it needs to be easy to maintain and you don't want to have regrets later.

Write a list of all the main areas you want to include in your plan: the patio, play area, lawn, flower borders, vegetable garden, greenhouse, compost area, washing line, and so on. All of these are interconnected and often you can't

A greenhouse set into the lawn can be an attractive feature in its own right. Hexagonal shapes are very useful where space is limited.

plan one without the other. Think about how you'll come in and out of the garden and how you'll get from A to B within it, particularly to the areas you'll visit on a regular basis, such as the clothes line or compost bin. On a copy of your plan, draw straight lines to all these from the place where you'll enter the garden. You can then experiment with making them curvy or winding or with right-angled changes of direction. Ensure that you include paths wherever they're needed, so no one is tempted to take a shortcut across a border or the lawn on a regular basis; on the other hand, do

A simple pergola and trellis separate the ornamental and utilitarian areas of the garden. A path leads to the end of the garden, reducing the temptation to walk across the grass.

try to keep their number to a minimum – you don't want a snakes-and-ladders effect in the garden and it might make sense to put certain areas closer together rather than creating another path.

Do a bit of research to discover how much space each fixed-size item might need (that is, the non-plant-related items). Go to a garden centre and find out the sizes of sheds and greenhouses, measure up your rotary dryer and dining room furniture (or, better still, a set of patio furniture at the garden centre). Assuming you've made a scale drawing of the garden, you can make scale drawings of all these items, or just draw boxes or shapes of the right size and label them

Are you one of those people who is unable to draw, can't visualize something unless it's physically right in front of you and has never been very good at judging distances? Don't despair. Get hold of a few good gardening magazines or books and have a look at what others have done before you; visit other people's gardens and take photographs. You'll soon know what you like and what you don't. Next, simply go out into the garden with a length of hosepipe or several metres of rope, some long bamboo canes or other pieces of wood and play with shapes for the lawn and the patio, the path and so on, remembering what was said earlier in this chapter. It may also help to look at the lawn and patio shapes on pages 26–7. Ideas will start to come thick and fast, and you can always change your mind as you go along.

If you can't visualize a design in your head or on paper, lay a hosepipe on the ground and play around with shapes until you're happy with the look, then create it for real.

If your plans for the garden go beyond a simple patio and lawn, you may need to contact your local planning department.

'patio', 'greenhouse', and so on. Cut them out and start moving them about on your drawing to find the best positions.

Be prepared to alter your ideas a few times before you feel you are getting near something that looks more or less suitable.

Making the plan a reality

By now you will have drawn and redrawn your plan several times, but at some point you need to call a halt and go with what you've got. At this stage, you can get the help of a builder or garden landscaper, who will give you an idea of cost and the timescale for the various elements that you want, or you can get out into the garden and begin marking out what goes where. Take it slowly and before you know it your garden will start to take shape.

First, you'll need to measure the new elements on your plan and multiply them to full scale. Make a note of the figures – a good place would be on the drawing itself.

Starting at the house end (or your baseline, if different), measure out and mark all the main features. To begin with, drive pegs into the ground (use lengths of battening with one end sharpened, or bamboo canes) to roughly indicate each area, then link the various shapes with rope or string.

Look at your handiwork from various places in the garden and house – go upstairs and look out of a window if necessary – and try to imagine what it will all look like in reality. Now is the time to make any final adjustments to the curve of a path, the corner of a patio and so on.

Mark out areas of lawn and flower bed using pegs and string. Be prepared to move them around a bit before you're completely satisfied.

Go back into the garden and start making more permanent markings. Trickle sand or spray landscaper's paint directly underneath the string or rope. Once you're happy with the layout of your proposed lawn or hard surface, you're ready to get digging. (For instructions of what to do next, see the relevant chapters.)

Use sand to mark final positions of the major elements of your garden. But remember, you can still change your mind later if you want.

Lawn and patio shapes

Your lawn, patio or deck will have an enormous impact on the overall appearance of the garden. Because they are comparatively large, these features can make or break a design, especially in a small garden, so it's very important to get them right. For example, depending on where they're sited and their size and shape, they instantly make the space look bigger, smaller, wider, narrower, formal, informal and so on.

To help you visualize their effect, think of a long, rectangular garden and then imagine a long, rectangular lawn in it. It's not that interesting, is it? And it accentuates the narrowness of the garden. But now imagine breaking the area up into two smaller lawns. Lines that run across a long, narrow space will make the area seem wider and shorter – it's not, of course, but it looks that way. What about introducing gentle curves instead of straight edges? Now the garden has gone from formal to informal in the blink of an eye. In small gardens, opt for fewer, larger elements – lots of small bits and bobs will make the area seem cluttered and busy; in bigger gardens, you need to think about breaking up large areas into smaller, more manageable chunks, otherwise they tend to seem rather distant and impersonal – mix small and large elements together.

The soft, undulating planting in this long border is accentuated by the curved lawn edging, which invites you to look slowly along it, enjoying the plants as you do so.

You could approach a patio or deck in the same way. Imagine the back wall of your house with a deck running all along it and jutting into the garden by about 4m (13ft). It may be practical, but it's not that exciting. But if you make the deck surface on two different levels, with the lower level extending a bit further out into the garden than the upper one, the effect is to invite you down onto the lower level and out into the garden. Add a decking path curving down the garden and you're well on the way to having a garden that is attractive as well as useful.

Go back to your sketch of the garden. Again, it makes sense to play around with different shapes and sizes for your lawn and patio or deck. Try a range of ideas and spend some time trying to imagine what they'd look like in reality.

The simple sketches shown on these pages take a long, rectangular garden and illustrate the different options and effects you can create depending on what you're looking for.

Lawn and patio shapes: the practicalities

When you draw your lawn or patio, be sure to consider the practicalities of the shape that you make. A lawn with lots of wiggly bits is much more difficult to mow and edge than one with straight edges – and 'difficult to mow' often translates as mowing badly or inefficiently. A lawn with long, sweeping curves, on the other hand, is fairly easy to mow, and the curves can be used to draw attention to particular areas. The same goes for the patio. It's all very well coming up with something in a complex geometric shape, but what about sweeping all those corners? Will you have to strim all round that hexagon each week just to keep the grass down?

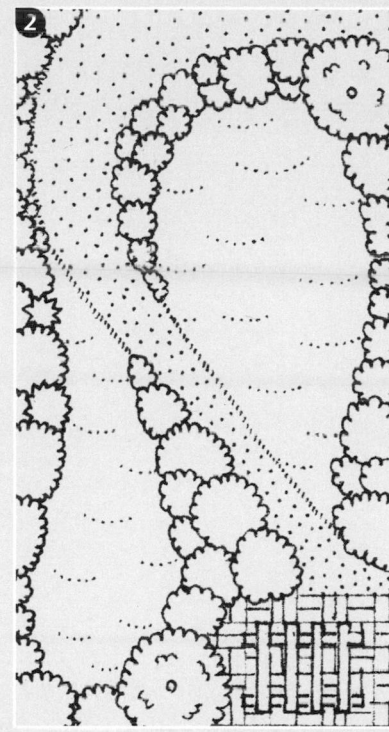

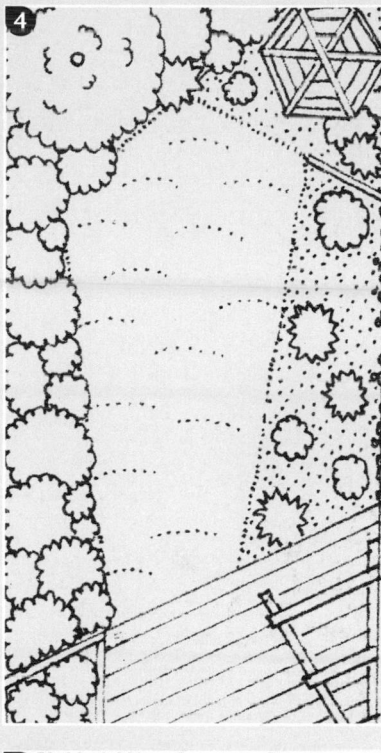
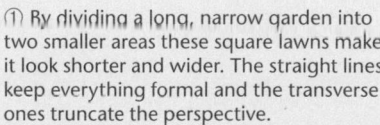
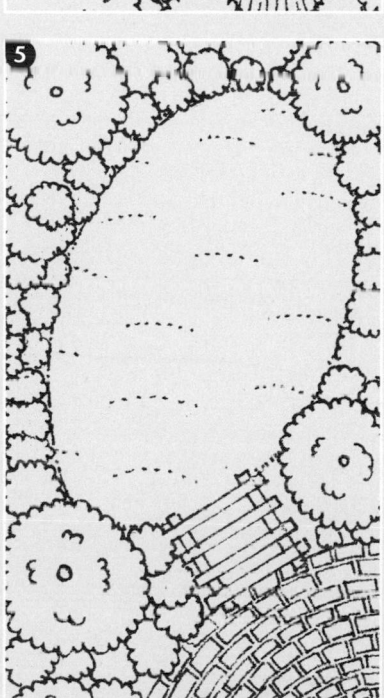

① By dividing a long, narrow garden into two smaller areas these square lawns make it look shorter and wider. The straight lines keep everything formal and the transverse ones truncate the perspective.

② A simple, flowing path guides you to the far end of the garden, but the loose, curved shapes of the lawns prevent it from seeming excessively long.

③ Large, geometric shapes placed in a small area interrupt your field of vision and make the space feel bigger. The curved lines of the circles soften the effect, while straight lines would look more dynamic.

④ A series of lines crossing the garden diagonally gives it a minimalist crispness while also making the space seem wider. The lawn fills nearly half the garden but doesn't dominate.

⑤ Sweeping curves create a country-garden feel even in this restricted area.

⑥ This lawn fills the garden but its curved lines prevent it from being dominant or making the garden seem overly long. The narrow areas are wide enough for a lawn mower to make at least two full passes.

Lawns

Many gardeners think nothing of spending hours weeding, planting, watering and feeding their borders yet devote little time to the lawn, giving the grass the occasional quick, ruthless, skinhead-style haircut. And yet, a neat, healthy lawn can be the first thing that catches the eye in a garden, giving an impression of beauty and order, even when the flower beds are less than perfect. So, getting the lawn right is important. If you're laying a new one, give it the best start possible; if you're faced with a lawn that's clearly struggling, there's plenty that you can do to improve the situation. Only occasionally do you have to concede defeat and start again.

What is a grass plant?

A lawn is made up of millions of individual grass plants. Unlike other plants, grasses and their relatives grow from the stem base rather than from the uppermost tip. This is why grass can be cut regularly and still keeps producing new growth. Another reason that grass is so resilient is that many types spread sideways at ground level and so produce bushy, multi-stemmed plants that tolerate being trampled underfoot.

A grass plant's anatomy

The long, narrow, strap-like grass leaves are tubular at first and form a sheath around the plant's stem. When it reaches a certain stage of development, the end section of the leaf opens up to form the characteristic flattened grass blade. Some leaves have a prominent groove (or rib) running along the centre of the leaf.

The grass flowerhead (inflorescence) is carried on a stem (culm) that is hollow and tubular with swollen joints (nodes) at regular intervals along its length. The flowers are pollinated by the wind, which blows the light, dusty pollen from one plant to another. This habit is what makes life so uncomfortable for hay-fever sufferers at certain times of the year. When pollination takes place, seeds are formed and these eventually drop to the ground to produce new grass plants.

The base of the individual grass plant is its centre of activity – all the growth that the plant produces emerges from this point.

Don't forget

When you buy grass seed, you'll be selecting a mixture of different grass types, not just one kind. There are lots of mixtures available, designed for different situations and depending on the type of lawn you require (*see* pages 40–1).

Types of grass plant

There are three distinct types of grass plant, recognized by their different habits of growth: rhizome-forming, tuft-forming and stolon-forming. Lawn seed usually contains a mixture of these three types.

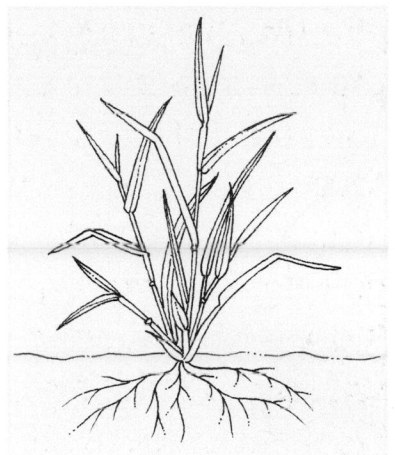

Tuft-forming grasses have a single root system. These grasses mainly spread by seed.

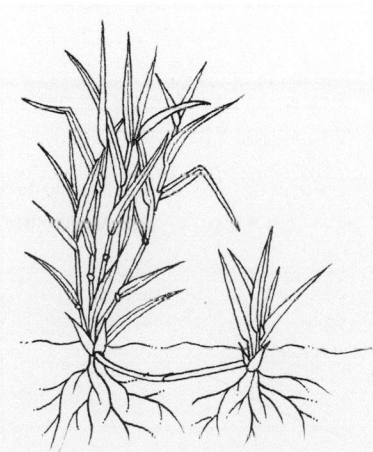

In a rhizome-forming grass the stem (rhizome) spreads below the surface and forms a new plant.

Rhizome-forming types send out creeping horizontal stems (rhizomes) below soil level; the rhizomes root at the stem nodes, each time forming a new plant, which then sends out its own rhizome, and so on. This type of grass is successful in dry soils.

Tuft-forming grasses grow a distinct group of stems from a single root system. They are upright in habit and have a limited spread.

Stolon-forming grasses send out creeping stems (stolons or runners) above soil level; these root at the nodes, forming more plants, which then send out their own stolons. Stoloniferous grasses are particularly successful in moist soils.

In stolon-forming grasses the stem (stolon) creeps above the surface.

Siting a lawn

When planning the shape and position of a new lawn, you'll need to take into consideration the suitability of the site. The amount of sun the area receives, the type of soil in your garden and good drainage are all key to a successful lawn. That's not to say that the site has to be perfect – there's plenty you can do to improve what nature has provided. But you do need to assess the area first, so you know what you're dealing with and can make improvements if necessary.

Lawn aspect

The direction your garden faces influences the amount of light your lawn receives and the kind of weather it has to deal with. Cold winds tend to come from the north and east, wet ones from the west and south west. Facing south means dealing with hot sun, while facing north may mean long periods without sun, especially in winter.

Being a horizontal surface, a lawn is less likely to be damaged by wind and weather than taller garden plants, but it will still be affected by deep shade and too much water, or the opposite – long sunny spells and drought. If your proposed lawn is going to be in full sun, you need to factor in strategies to stop it turning brown in summer. In practice, this means leaving it longer when you

mow (so that the leaves shade the roots) and watering when necessary. If, on the other hand, it's going to receive lots of rain and you can see that the drainage isn't good, you'll need to attend to this before laying or sowing the lawn (*see* pages 33–4).

Shade and drought

It's best not to site your lawn in a very shady part of the garden, because grass is a hardworking plant that needs plenty of sun to survive. Buildings and structures such as fences or walls may shade

This gently sloping, well-drained site, with areas that are shaded for only part of the day, is ideal for growing a healthy lawn. Lawns on steeply sloping sites are best avoided as they will be extremely difficult to mow.

the site for part of the day and they may also produce a rain shadow (*see* below), which means a lack of water in the area affected. Watch how the sun moves around during the course of the day. If the area gets about half a day's sunlight, this type of shade may not present problems. Similarly, it is possible to cope with smaller rain shadows, especially if you provide a little extra water in the area when needed.

Trees that overhang the lawn are more likely to create permanent problems. The shade they cast can make growth difficult for the grass, and lack of light will lead to elongated, weak shoots that are easy prey for fungal diseases (*see* pages 63–4). Also, falling leaves in autumn can smother the grass, excluding

The position of a lawn plays a key part in its success. An open site that gets sun for much of the day is best. Planting trees at the back of borders rather than in the lawn tends to reduce the number of problems.

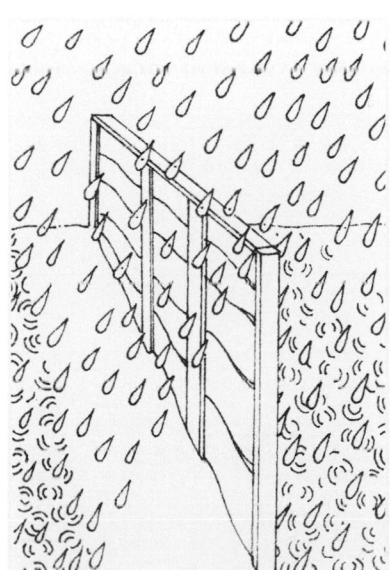

Fences and walls create rain shadows: soil that is sheltered from prevailing rain will always be very dry. It's unlikely to be suitable for grass unless you're prepared to water regularly.

light and heating up as they decay, leading to fungal problems and rot. Trees can cause other problems too – they're thirsty plants, so the ground beneath them can be very dry; conversely, after heavy rain they may drip water onto the lawn and create localized wet spots. If the trees belong to you, consider some judicious pruning to lighten the canopy and reduce areas of heavy shade. You could also rejig your lawn so it's away from the heaviest shade. If the trees belong to a neighbour, you may need to ask if you can do some pruning, and again redefine the edges of the lawn away from the darkest areas.

Deciduous trees that overhang the lawn can pose real problems, including fallen leaves, which block light and cause diseases.

If you're unsure of your soil type, go out into the garden on a dry day, pick up a handful, give it a squeeze, then open your hand. Take a close look at the colour and texture of the soil.

① Sandy soil will slip through your fingers and feels rough and gritty.

② Clay soil may be greyish rather than brown. It will form a clod in your hand and feels sticky.

③ Peaty soil is dark, soft and spongy. If it's wet you might get some drops of water out of it as you squeeze.

④ Chalky soil is pale or greyish brown, which should give you a clue before you squeeze. It's slightly gritty with white fragments in it and is crumbly so will not form a clump.

⑤ Loam is mid- to dark brown and feels soft and crumbly. Depending on how dry it is, it might form a soft clump.

Your garden soil

Understanding the type of soil you have in your garden is vital for the success of your lawn. Depending on where you live, your garden soil will be made up of varying amounts of loam, sand, chalk (limestone), clay and/or peat. Luckily, grass will grow on any of these soils, but it's helpful to know what type of soil you have, as well as its quality and condition, as this will determine how much preparation you put in (*see* pages 36–8), your choice of seed or turf, whether or not you'll have drainage problems (*see* pages 33–4) and how you maintain your lawn once established. Garden soil usually consists of a layer of fertile topsoil and a layer of considerably less fertile subsoil.

Sandy soil Water drains quickly through sand, taking nutrients with it as it goes, so although it is a reasonable surface for grass, a lawn on sandy soil will need regular feeding and occasional watering.

Clay soil Heavy and fertile, clay has the advantage of retaining moisture and nutrients. However, drainage can be difficult on clay and the result may be compaction of the soil and drainage problems.

Chalky soil Grass grows quite happily on chalk: it is fertile and drains well, but it can be shallow.

Loam This drains well, is relatively fertile, and is easy to improve by digging in organic matter. Grass thrives in loam.

Find out your soil's pH

In some areas you can make deductions about your soil – for instance, if you have chalky soil you can assume it's alkaline and if it's peaty it will have a high acid content. Otherwise, the easiest way to find out the pH of your soil is to get a kit from a garden centre; these are cheap, quick to use and accurate enough for gardeners. Take the soil sample from a few centimetres down, so that the influence of local factors such as rainfall is reduced, and follow the instructions on the pack. Compare the final colour of your sample against the chart supplied with the kit. Changing the pH of your soil to make it more alkaline can be done by adding lime or chalk, but it is more difficult to acidify it. Any changes you make will be short-lived, so generally it's best to work with what you have.

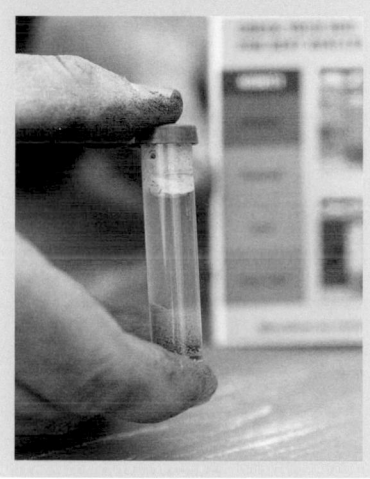

A sloping garden has been terraced to minimize drainage problems that would result in rainwater collecting at the bottom of the slope.

Peaty soil This is found in moorland environments and is naturally wet and low in nutrients. Grass will grow on peaty soil, but you need to ensure your drainage is good and provide regular feeds.

Soil pH

Soil may be alkaline or acid; this alkalinity and acidity is measured on a scale called a pH scale, which goes from 1 to 14, with 1 being very acid and 14 being very alkaline. Some plants, such as camellias and rhododendrons, have a marked preference for acidic conditions; others prefer alkaline conditions. There are various grass species that are adapted to grow in acid or alkaline conditions, but most grass plants favour neutral to slightly acidic soil (pH 6.0–6.5).

Drainage

Good drainage is essential for a healthy lawn. Ideally, rainwater should percolate downwards through the soil away from the surface, being taken up by plant roots as necessary, and ending up in the water table below. For this to happen, the soil needs a good structure that allows the water to pass through. If anything has happened to interfere with the structure – for example, if new topsoil has been introduced into the garden during construction work – this may not happen and the water will be slow to drain.

The soil type will also influence drainage, particularly clay and sand (*see* opposite). Other factors that affect drainage, or at least make your garden damp, include a high water table or a spring rising in the garden. In areas without mains sewage, the soakaway from the septic tank may cause parts of your garden to be damper than others, and a garden that is at the bottom of a hill or in a valley may receive more than its fair share of water, due

Don't forget

You should never walk on your soil in wet weather, because your weight may compact the surface into a solid layer that will dry to form a hard, impenetrable crust and will cause drainage problems.

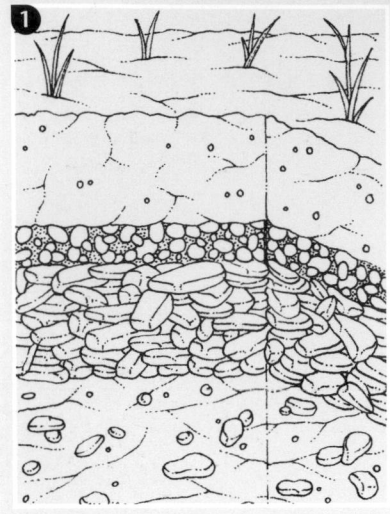
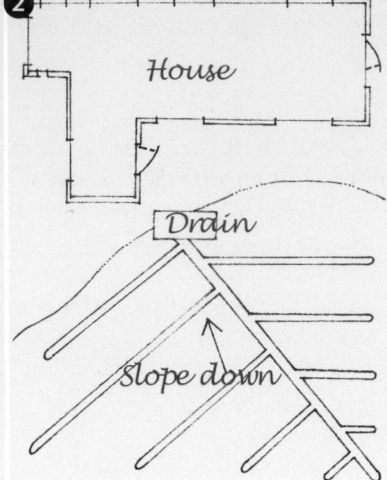

If you have really bad drainage in the garden it may well be worth installing a drainage system before sowing or laying a new lawn.

① A simple soakaway system improves drainage on a flat site. Excavate the lawn area to a depth of 35cm (14in) and spread a layer of rubble 15cm (6in) deep. On top of this add a layer of gravel or coarse sand 5cm (2in) deep, then replace the topsoil so that it is about 15cm (6in) deep all over.

On a sloping site, soakaway pits with a greater depth of rubble and sand can be used. They can be sited in the lowest part of the garden, alowing water to trickle away without sitting on your lawn.

② A herringbone drainage system needs to be installed by a professional water engineer. Drainage pipes and rubble are laid underground. They're connected to an existing drainage system and excess water is taken away before it can cause a problem.

to drainage from higher up. If the problem seems to have appeared suddenly, don't rule out a leaking water-supply pipe, which – with water costs being what they are – would be well worth fixing.

Symptoms of poor drainage

In a garden with poor drainage the soil may be compacted, particularly if you garden on clay soil or an area that has recently been under construction. During the building of a new house and garden, the land takes a lot of punishment: the ground is driven over by various vehicles as they transport building materials around, which compacts the soil and forms a solid crust over the surface. When the building is complete, rather than go over the area and break up the crust, builders often simply put a layer of additional soil over the top. You move in, plant up the area and soon have a lovely garden. But after a few weeks or

months, depending on the weather and the time of year, the plants and grass start dying and you hear a distinct squelching sound when you walk across the lawn. This means the crust that has formed is preventing steady drainage.

Poor drainage also shows up as moss or algae on lawns, yellowing of the grass as its roots die from sitting in water for too long, reed-type grasses growing in shady corners, and puddling of water after rain.

Improving drainage in a lawn

If the ground is compacted before you create a new lawn, it's a relatively simple job to fix it by thorough digging and forking over of the soil. It's a good idea to follow the single digging method (*see* page 37) if your soil is heavy. If you're in a newly constructed area, you'll need to fork over builders' rubble and remove large fragments of concrete, bricks and so on.

Once a lawn is established, localized wet spots that occur after heavy rain can be dealt with by spiking the grass with a garden fork (*see* pages 57–8).

If you have very poor drainage, are unsure of the cause and don't want your lawn to become a bog garden, it makes good sense to call in a professional water engineer. They will be able to advise you on the reasons for the problem and any possible solutions. If you have really bad drainage they may recommend a herringbone-pattern drainage system (*see* box, above).

Don't forget

Imported topsoil, often used in newly created gardens, can sometimes cause drainage problems in lawns because its fertility and drainage rates won't match those of the soil beneath. However, you can help by forking the old and new soil together. Also, the organisms living in the soil will soon start to mix the layers together, so the situation will gradually improve over time.

Tools and equipment

A set of good-quality tools is vital, whether you are preparing the site for a new lawn or caring for an established one. Some of these tools are essential, others are more specialized and you could buy them over time.

Spade Essential for digging the ground to reduce compaction before sowing seed or laying turf, shifting soil and turf, and for remedial work on an established lawn. (See pages 36–8, 65.)

Fork Useful for preparing the ground before creating a lawn (see pages 36–7) as well as general maintenance. Spiking the lawn with a fork helps to aerate the soil and relieve surface drainage problems (see pages 57–8).

Garden rake After preparing the soil, it will need pulling roughly level with a large-tined rake (see pages 37–8). If you are laying turf, you can also use it for tamping down the turves after you've laid them.

Spring-tine (fan) rake A special lawn rake known as a spring-tine or fan rake is used to remove thatch, dead moss and leaves from an established lawn, making it easier for air and water to get to the soil beneath (see page 57). It may be used to level the ground when preparing the site for a new lawn, but a standard garden rake is better.

Lawn mower An essential piece of equipment for cutting grass on any lawn. There is a vast selection to choose from, including petrol-operated, electric or manually driven types (see pages 54–5).

Half-moon cutter An invaluable tool for cutting turf pieces to shape and for creating a neat, well-defined edge (see pages 44, 45–6, 65).

Long-handled edging shears These are useful for trimming overhanging grass at the lawn edges, giving a neat, finished look (see page 45).

Watering devices There is a range of watering equipment designed for the lawn, including different watering cans, sprinklers and hoses (see page 52).

Hollow-tined aerator A simple but effective tool for relieving compaction in the lawn's upper surface (see top right and page 58).

Strimmer An electric or petrol-operated strimmer is good for cutting grass in awkward areas that are not easily reached by a mower, such as around trees or shrubs.

Distributor This is not essential, but it helps in the accurate dispersal of fertilizer, grass seed and granular weedkiller (see page 50).

Garden roller Once grass seed starts growing it's a good idea to roll the surface to resettle the soil, firm seedlings and cause branching at the base. If you don't have one you could tread instead (see page 38).

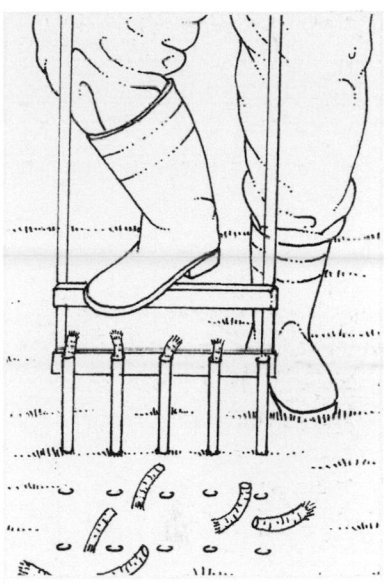

A hollow-tined aerator penetrates the turf and removes cores of soil and grass, opening up compacted turf. The soil plugs may be collected up for adding to the compost bin.

Canes Bamboo canes are useful for marking out the site for a new lawn and for working out how much seed to sow (see box, page 42).

Garden line A line in a bright colour, such as orange, enables you to see it easily. Use it to mark out the lawn perimeter.

Wooden boards When laying turf, you need to work on boards so you don't damage the grass (see page 44). They also help to firm the turf you've already laid.

Stiff broom or besom A broom is useful for sweeping away leaves and piles of earth caused by worms, ants and mining bees (see page 62).

Preparing the site for a new lawn

You've probably already realized that there's no shortcut to having a good lawn. Proper preparation leads to healthy grass growth, but lack of it can leave the grass struggling to survive. There are two ways to make a lawn: sowing seed or laying turf (*see* pages 39–44). Both will give a good result. Whichever method you choose, you'll need to prepare the site in the same way before you start.

Clearing the site

On pages 18–25 you were shown how to design, plan and mark out an area with pegs, string and sand before creating a new area of lawn or hard surfacing. Now's the time to do the heavy work. First, clear the area of any previous occupants such as trees, shrubs and flower beds.

If there's already a neglected lawn in place, you'll need to get rid of the existing grass before you can start again. There are two ways you can do this: either undercut the turf, separating it from the soil's surface with a flat spade (make sure that you don't take too much soil with it); or, you could kill off the grass using a herbicide. If you choose the first option, you can turn the old turves into a valuable source of topsoil (*see* box, right); if the latter, you'll have to wait between six and eight weeks before sowing or laying turf. Spot-treat or dig out weeds that appear during this time (*see* pages 60–1).

Digging is the key to improving almost every site. This stony soil will also need thorough raking to ensure that the grass has an even surface to grow on.

Making a turf stack

To make topsoil from your old turves, stack them upside down in a bricklaying pattern in a quiet corner of the garden. Within six months to a year, the grass will have rotted down and you'll have reasonably fertile soil.

Other surfaces, such as paving, concrete or brick, will need to be completely removed, including any hardcore foundation. This is heavy work, and you may prefer to have it done by an outside contractor. Old paving slabs, blocks or bricks can be lifted and reused elsewhere, but concrete will need breaking up before it's taken away.

Digging

Once you've cleared the site, it's time to start digging. It sounds like hard work – and it is. You may be tempted to skip this stage, but for the sake of your future lawn, please don't! Digging is one of the most important steps to a healthy, happy, long-lasting lawn. There are various ways to dig – some are harder work than others. If your soil is in good shape, simple digging will be fine for preparing the site for a lawn, but if you have very heavy or light soil, it will be worth doing a really thorough job using the single digging method (*see* below). If all this sounds like too much hard work, you could hire a rotavator, although these baulk at really hard ground, too.

Simple digging
This basic method involves digging the whole area over to the depth of a single spade blade, turning it over and breaking it up as you go. With heavy or stony soil, you can also use a fork for this process. This type of digging prepares the surface layer for sowing seed, but it does nothing to affect the lower level, so it's recommended only where drainage is already good or where you know that the soil has been well cultivated in the past. For example, if you're making a lawn in an area that was previously flower borders or a vegetable patch, simple digging will nearly always suffice.

Single digging
A more systematic method, this is good preparation for areas that haven't been cultivated for a long time and where drainage is poor.

Work across the site, opening a trench, removing the soil into a barrow or a heap out of the way, then using a fork (or even a pickaxe) to break up the lower layer. Use the soil from the next trench to fill the previous one and so on across the area until you've dug the last trench. Fill this with the soil from the first. In the process of single digging, you can add soil improvers – well-rotted compost or farmyard manure – if needed. If the drainage is really poor, such as in a heavy clay soil, forking this in or adding gravel or hardcore to the layer below will help the upper layers to drain quickly.

Levelling the site
A level lawn is a lovely lawn, whereas high and low patches result in areas of scalping (where the grass is removed down to the roots) and long grass, which are not at all pretty. It's much more difficult to get rid of lumps and dips when the grass is growing, so spend plenty of

HOW TO single dig

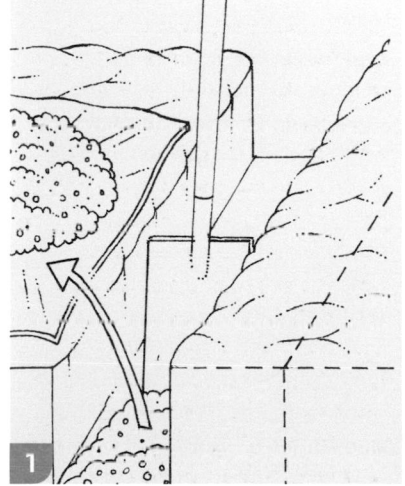

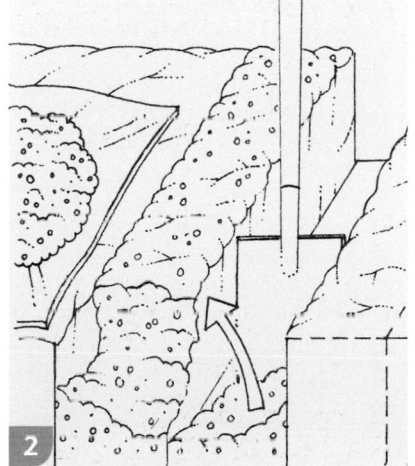

1 Dig a trench to about one spade's depth and width. Place the soil you've dug on some thick plastic sheeting and set aside as you will need it later. Remove any weeds as you go along.

2 Dig another trench next to the first and put the soil from it into the first trench. Add any soil improvers if necessary (*see* above). Continue in this way until you get to the final trench.

3 Fill the final trench, which will now be empty, with the soil on the plastic sheeting that was taken from the first trench. Go over the whole area and break up any lumps with the spade or a garden fork.

After digging, draw a garden rake across the exposed soil in order to level the site and remove obstacles such as large stones and other debris from the surface.

time getting the soil level now. Be really fussy about it, because as the ground settles uneven areas will appear in any case.

After digging, rake the area level and remove surface stones, old roots and so on. Stand back regularly to check the site from different parts of the garden. Even out any particularly high or low spots by transferring soil from one to the other.

Levelling the topsoil

The topsoil is the fertile layer of soil. It's like the cream on the milk and is what the grass will grow best in, so don't risk mixing it with the subsoil (which will look and feel different). If the soil levels have to be altered by more than 5–8cm (2–3in) for levelling purposes, the best approach is to scrape off the topsoil and stack it away from the area being landscaped. Carry out the levelling work required, working with the subsoil until the levels are almost correct, then bring back the topsoil and spread it evenly over the area to cover the subsoil. This should create the best possible root zone for the new lawn.

If your lawn area is very uneven or shallow – that is, if the topsoil is less than 15–22cm (6–9in) deep – you may need to bring in new topsoil. Always mix the imported

After rough raking, treading is vital to create a firm bed for the seed or turf. Finally, you'll rake the area over to make it really level and smooth for sowing.

soil with the existing soil on the site, because no two soils have identical properties. Mixing will also ensure that drainage will occur through all the levels.

Feeding

When the soil is level, it's a good idea to add some grass fertilizer, sprinkling it at the recommended rate, before going on to the next step. This will ensure it's thoroughly mixed in to the soil, ready for the new grass to use as it grows.

Firming the soil

In between the rough raking to level the surface and the final raking that will produce the seedbed finish, you need to firm the soil enough to stop it settling too much the first time it gets rained on. This involves walking over the whole area using tiny, close steps with all your weight on your heels. Don't tread on a wet day or when you're in a hurry. Take your time and be particular about covering every inch. Yes, your neighbours may think you've gone potty, but you'll have the last laugh when you have a beautiful lawn.

Final raking

After treading, you'll need to rake again to even out any spots that settled as you walked over the area and to remove stones. But here let me offer a word of caution. The longer you rake, the more stones will come to the surface. You are not aiming to create a fine dust, more a surface that looks like the top of a fruit crumble, while leaving the under surface firm enough to enable the grass to root strongly and deeply.

Grass seed or turf?

When it comes to laying a new lawn, you have the choice of whether to sow seed or lay turf. The decision is really a matter of convenience, time, finances and what you want from the lawn.

Timescale and suitability

Seed is much cheaper than turf, and it's very quick and easy to sow, but it takes time to grow and tends to remain dormant if the weather conditions aren't right for germination. When it does appear, it takes about six weeks to reach the stage where you can walk on it (by which time weeds will have grown up alongside the new grass plants) and you shouldn't expose it to heavy use for the first 12 months. Turf, on the other hand, creates an instant lawn – well, it might take you a day or two to lay it – and it can be walked on in two or three weeks. It also covers the ground completely, so suppressing weed growth to a greater extent than seed.

There is a range of turf types available, but this is limited compared to the variety of seed mixtures, each formulated for specific situations and uses including family, shady, and drought-tolerant (*see* pages 40–1). If you can put a tick next to any of these specific requirements, you might be advised to choose seed.

If they are to grow into a thing of beauty, both turf- and seed-based lawns need very careful looking after in their first few months and regular attention thereafter.

Maintenance

Both seed and turf need a certain amount of cosseting during their first few months. Before it has anchored itself into the soil beneath, turf is particularly susceptible to drought and needs regular watering if rainfall is low. It's important not to let the turves dry out as they'll shrink and gaps will appear all over the lawn. If they dry out too much, the grass will die.

Seed is most vulnerable before it germinates, because it's a popular food with birds; they also like to take dust baths in the exposed soil, which will disturb the emerging seedlings. Like turf, seed needs watering in dry spells (*see* page 42).

Choosing and using seed

When buying lawn seed it's important to consider the type that's best suited to your garden and your individual needs. The best lawns are created using a combination of grasses that have different habits of growth. While individually these grasses might not produce a wholly satisfactory lawn, when blended they complement each other.

Buying grass seed

Grass seed is nearly always sold in mixes that have been specially formulated for particular situations. There's a vast choice available, so you should work out exactly what your requirements are before you buy. First, consider what the conditions are like in your garden (shady, sunny, damp, dry) and what type of lawn you want (luxury, hardwearing, drought-tolerant, and so on). That way, you can get the right seed mixture and it will be more likely to grow well. Just a few of the seed mixtures available are described here.

Luxury mixtures These result in the classic green, velvety carpet desired by so many. A well-tended luxury lawn will steal the show, but it cannot withstand heavy use and needs regular, careful maintenance to remain looking beautiful. Luxury-grade mixtures include fine-leaved, compact grasses such as hard fescue (*Festuca longifolia*), chewings fescue (*F. rubra* subsp. *commutata*) and sheep's fescue (*F. ovina*).

All it needs is a good eye and a steady hand to broadcast grass seed, though measuring and marking the area will produce a more even result.

Lawn seed mixtures: the pros and cons

LUXURY GRASS SEED MIXTURE
Produces a beautiful rich, neat green carpet and is highly ornamental.

BUT...
- A luxury lawn will not stand up to heavy wear so is unsuitable for a family garden or areas of heavy traffic.
- It will not tolerate neglect.
- Luxury mixtures are more expensive than hardwearing ones.
- Luxury-grade lawns are slower-growing than hardwearing mixtures.
- Bumps and other irregularities show up more than on hardwearing mixtures.

HARDWEARING GRASS SEED MIXTURE
Highly resilient, tolerates neglect, is quicker to establish, more forgiving and less expensive than a luxury lawn.

BUT...
- It doesn't have the luxuriant 'bowling green' appearance.
- Some mixtures can grow too quickly, so regular mowing is essential.
- Some inferior mixtures can die off with close mowing.

MIXTURE CONTAINING MICROCLOVER
Eco-friendly, sustainable option: drought-tolerant and comparatively low-maintenance; microclover keeps grass green without using fertilizer. Less prone to weed growth and diseases.

BUT...
- Microclover will dominate the lawn at certain times of the year.
- It does not produce as neat a sward as many all-grass mixtures, especially when viewed at close quarters.

Hardwearing mixtures Also known as utility-grade or general-purpose formulations, hardwearing mixtures are ideal for family gardens. They stand up to children's games, bicycles and plenty of foot traffic, although they're still subject to wear if overused or under-tended. They're made up of thick, closely knit turf based around perennial ryegrass (*Lolium perenne*), used for its strength and ability to recover, and broad-leaved turf grasses.

Shady mixtures Many grasses require sun so if your garden is shady you'll have to choose a special blend. Shade-tolerant mixtures include hard fescue (*Festuca longifolia*), browntop bent (*Agrostis capillaris* syn. *A. tenuis*) and creeping red fescue (*Festuca rubra* subsp. *rubra*).

Microclover and grass mix Mixtures containing microclover are a relatively new and environmentally friendly alternative to an all-grass lawn. Resembling clover but with smaller leaves, microclover has

For a family garden that takes a lot of wear, select a resilient seed mixture that contains plenty of ryegrass.

many advantages: it's very drought-resistant and can smother most other lawn weeds. Also, as the roots decay, the clover releases nitrogen, which fertilizes the grass and keeps it looking green year round. The effect will be lower maintenance and lower cost, and fewer chemicals need to be used. Unlike other grass-alternative plants (*see* page 111), microclover can be clipped with a conventional mower. Never use ordinary weedkiller with these mixes as it will also kill the microclover.

Sowing grass seed

Sow grass seed in late summer to early autumn or in late spring. The end of the year is most likely to be better because long, dry spells are rarer at this time, but spring is also a perfectly acceptable time for sowing if the weather isn't particularly cold or dry. Choose a time when the soil is moist but not waterlogged, and when the weather is reasonably warm but not too hot.

Microclover combined with grass seed makes an excellent green, drought-resistant lawn.

Protect the seed

Make every attempt to keep birds off the seed until it germinates (seven to ten days in warm weather, but up to three weeks if you sow in spring). The seed may have a bird repellent in it, but otherwise lay

Grass seed will usually start to germinate one to three weeks after sowing, depending on the weather.

twiggy pea-sticks across the area to discourage dust-bathing. You could decorate them with something shiny, such as strips of parcel ribbon, aluminium foil or old CDs. Or, with a smallish area, you could lay horticultural fleece across it – this provides warmth and also allows light through for germination. Peg it down at the edges to ensure it doesn't sail off in the breeze. Avoid netting, which can trap birds.

Watering

It's best not to water grass seed before it germinates – if you do, you'll have to continue watering regularly or the seedlings will die, whereas if you leave it the seed will simply remain dormant until the conditions are suitable for growth. However, once the seed has started to germinate, it's vital to provide some water in dry spells to keep the young seedlings going. Water well but gently, ensuring the soil is thoroughly soaked. If you sprinkle water lightly across the surface you'll do more harm than good, as the grass roots will not be encouraged to grow deeply in search of moisture.

Rolling or treading

After sowing, keep off the lawn completely for at least six weeks – or until the seedling grass is about 3cm (1½in) high – then roll it (you can hire a roller from your local hire shop if you don't have one);

Try to keep off newly sown lawns for as long as possible, ideally six months or so.

alternatively, you can tread over the ground instead. This causes branching of the plants right down at the base, which makes the lawn look much thicker almost instantly. It also resettles any soil that was lifted with the germinating grass and firms the seedlings into the soil. Pick off any stones that have risen to the surface before you roll or tread.

The first cut

Try not to walk on the lawn at all if you can help it for the first few months – for best results, it shouldn't be subjected to heavy traffic for about six months. You may notice weeds germinating in the new lawn while the grass is still starting to grow, but don't worry about them. Most will die when you begin to mow.

The lawn is ready for its first cut when the grass reaches about 5cm (2in) high. Set the blades high, so you remove only the top third of the growth (*see* page 53).

Don't forget

Put any leftover seed in an airtight glass jar and store it in a cool, dark place. You can then use it to fill in any bare patches later.

Don't forget

You can buy a combination of lawn seed and fertilizer, which will provide your young lawn with all its nutritional requirements for the first few months of its life.

Alternative sowing methods

If you're concerned about sowing the lawn unevenly, there are several alternative sowing methods you could try. Whatever method you use, you need to prepare the seed bed and rake after sowing in the same way (*see* pages 36–8).

One method involves making a frame out of four 1m (40in) bamboo canes strapped together. Place the frame at the edge of the seed bed, weigh out the amount of seed required for 1 square metre (details will be given on the seed packet), then scatter this evenly within the square. Once you've sown one area, move the frame over the lawn surface to the next square metre and repeat the process until you've covered the whole lawn, then rake it lightly in. A faster method would be to use the bamboo frame simply as a test square. Measure the required amount of seed and scatter it in the square, as before. If you feel confident that you can judge the area and density accurately by sight, you could then copy the effect over the whole lawn.

Another sowing method is to use a machine called a distributor (*see* page 50), sowing half the seed in one direction and half at right angles to this.

Choosing and using turf

If you're buying turf, always seek out a reputable dealer. Cheap turf will be a false economy, as it may have come from anywhere (even a meadow that's about to be built on) and you'll be importing weeds as well as some very coarse grasses that will be difficult to eradicate later. If possible, inspect the turf before you buy it. It should be a healthy green, not too long and weed free.

Buying turf

Turf is sold by the square metre. It's usually delivered in strips measuring about 100 x 30cm (40 x 12in). Ideally, arrange to have it delivered just before you want to lay it. It will be rolled up into neat bundles when it arrives, and it's important to unroll it as soon as possible so it doesn't begin to turn yellow (through lack of light) or go mouldy (as the lack of air and increased heat cause fungal spores to flourish). Don't leave it rolled up for longer than a couple of days. It's a good idea to water the rolls you don't immediately need.

Laying turf

Turf can be laid almost any time of the year as long as the ground isn't too dry, frozen or soaking. Autumn and spring are best. Summer can be too dry (unless you're prepared to water heavily and regularly) and it's probably best to avoid doing it in winter as it's often too cold or wet.

When laying turf (*see* page 44), stagger the joints between the turves and try to place any offcuts in

Good turf consists of fine-quality grass on a fertile soil base. It comes in rolls and should be laid as soon as possible. Turf must not crack when rolled up and should show healthy green grass when unrolled.

Water is vital for newly laid turf. The grass roots have been severed and exposed to the elements for at least 24 hours so they need all the help they can get to recover from the shock.

Don't forget

When laying turf, don't step all over your carefully prepared surface. Use wooden planks on top of the newly laid turves; they also help to firm the turf down to make good contact with the soil.

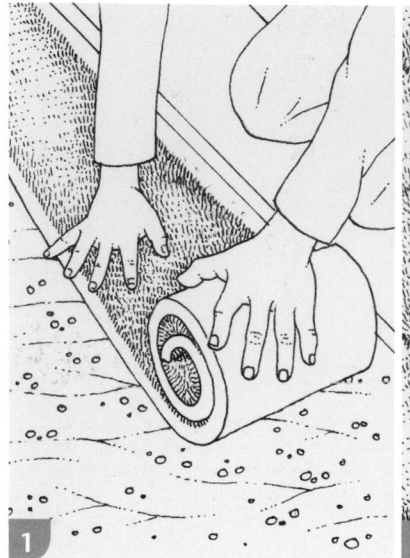

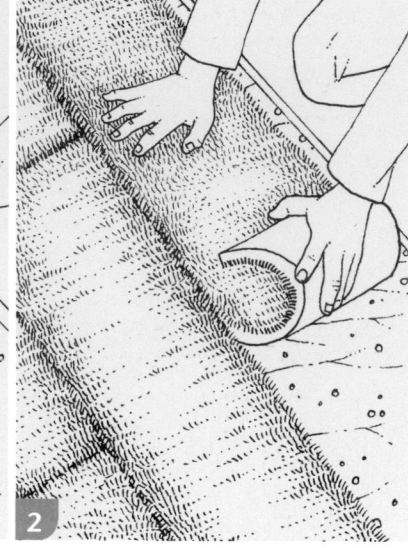

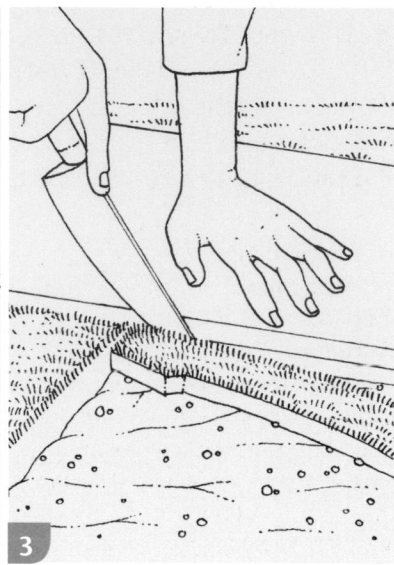

1 Prepare the ground thoroughly so that it's level before you lay the turves (*see* pages 36–8). Kneeling on a plank (never on the prepared soil or newly laid turf), lay the first roll of turf in a straight line and pat it down lightly in contact with the soil using the head of a garden rake. Add the next roll, butting the short ends together and, again, pat it into position.

2 When you've finished the first row, start on the second row. Stagger the joints between the turves like joints in brickwork. Repeat until the whole area is covered with turves. The final pieces laid at the lawn edges should be large pieces. Always try to have the small offcuts in the centre of the lawn, never at the edge, where they will receive more wear.

3 Use an old kitchen knife or half-moon cutter to trim any excess turf and to form the shape of the lawn – either straight or curved – then sweep the surface of the turves to remove debris, and water well. Keep off the grass until it has rooted down into the soil. You can test this by peeling back the corner of turves. If you can't lift them, then the grass has rooted down.

the centre of the lawn rather than around the edges, where they're much more likely to dry out or become dislodged.

Aftercare

In damp weather there will be no need to water the turf, but in dry spells, turn on a lawn sprinkler every few days so the turf does not have a chance to dry out and shrink. Alternatively, you can use a perforated hose (also known as a seep hose), which has small holes all along its length and is designed to supply water with a steady drip

straight into the soil. The water needs to soak through the turf and into the soil below; it's particularly important to keep the bottom of the turf and the surface of the soil moist to encourage the grass roots to penetrate into the soil as quickly as possible. This method of watering is better than using a sprinkler, which wets the surface of the turf but, unless left in place for a considerable time, may not penetrate to any depth.

Keep off the new turf for about two or three weeks if possible to give the grass a chance to establish and root into the ground.

The grass will be ready for its first cut when it reaches about 5cm (2in) high. Set the mower blades high so you remove only the top third of the growth. Once the turf has established in position (about six weeks), you can apply a weed-and-feed preparation all over if you notice any weeds starting to come through (*see* pages 60–1).

Don't forget

If there are bumps or hollows in your newly turfed lawn, don't try pushing them down with the back of a spade. Instead, lift the turf and remove or add extra soil (*see* page 65).

Creating perfect edges

If there's one thing that's guaranteed to ruin the effect of a lawn, it's tatty edges. An irregular, uncut edge will make even the best-kept lawn look untidy, no matter how neat the stripes or how well the moss and weeds are controlled. For the best effect, re-cut the edges of the lawn once a year and trim the edges at least once a week while the grass is actively growing, and preferably every time the lawn is mown.

Trim overhanging grass at the lawn edges regularly using long-handled edging shears. Ideally, do this after mowing the lawn.

We tend to think of a lawn as something static, but in actual fact the ground is moving very slightly all the time. One of the reasons for this is compaction of the soil. We walk on the lawn far more than any other part of the garden; as a result, the passage of our feet (and weight) pushes the soil under the lawn outwards as well as downwards. Also, the grass roots develop and spread outwards. This means that, over a period of time, the lawn gets larger and the borders around the lawn get narrower. The process does not happen at the same rate around the whole edge of the lawn, so it gradually takes on an uneven and irregular shape. Where the edges have broken down, the grass may start spreading into the borders and both the lawn and the borders begin to look unkempt. It also makes both more difficult to look after.

Re-cutting the lawn edge

The good news is that if you re-cut the lawn edge once a year you can quickly restore a semblance of order – like mowing, re-cutting lawn edges is a sure-fire way to make the whole garden look spruce again.

Aim to start with a fresh, sharp edge each spring – look upon edging as the first step in your annual maintenance routine.

There are two tools necessary for edging work: long-handled edging shears and a half-moon cutter. The shears have cutting blades set at an angle of 90 degrees to the handles, making it possible to trim the grass from a standing position. Some are fitted with a small scoop or pocket on the side of the blade to catch the clippings as they fall. A half-moon cutter consists of a metal or plastic, semi-circular blade fitted onto a long wooden or metal shaft. It is used in a slicing or rocking motion to cut through the soil and grass roots to create a new edge.

There's nothing quite like a neatly mown lawn with a crisp, sharp edge to set off the early flowers in your garden borders.

Don't forget

Re-cut the edge only once a year, otherwise your lawn will shrink to the size of a postage stamp; for the rest of the year, make do with trimming.

How to re-cut a lawn edge

To cut back a straight lawn edge, mark out where you want to make the edge using a taut garden line. Place a wooden board on the ground adjacent to your marked line. Stand on the board (to stop it moving) and insert the blade of the half-moon cutter vertically into the lawn, parallel with the board, until the top of the blade is level with the surface of the lawn. If the cut piece doesn't come out readily, slide a spade horizontally along the flower border soil to expose the new edge.

If you want a curved edge to your lawn, a hosepipe makes an ideal template. Set the hosepipe into the shape you require, then sprinkle sand along the edge to act as a marker before cutting or do it by eye, shifting the hosepipe slightly back out of the way as you go (*see* page 25).

Trimming edges

When you clip your lawn edges, you're tidying up the parts that the mower can't reach, so most people prefer to do it after mowing to ensure a neat finish. Hopefully, you will have well-defined edges from re-cutting on an annual basis; if so, trimming is simply a matter of aligning the lower blade of the long-handled edging shears (*see* page 45) against the vertical part of the edge and holding it still while you bring the handle of the upper blade up to

HOW TO repair a broken edge

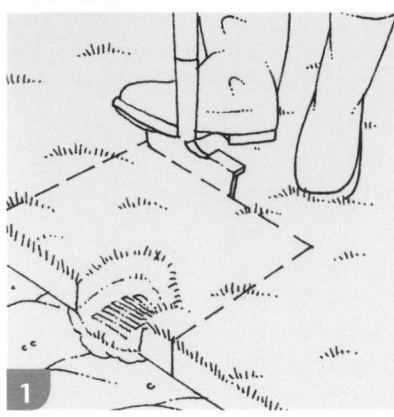

1 Using a half-moon cutter, cut around a square of turf that includes the damaged or broken edge.

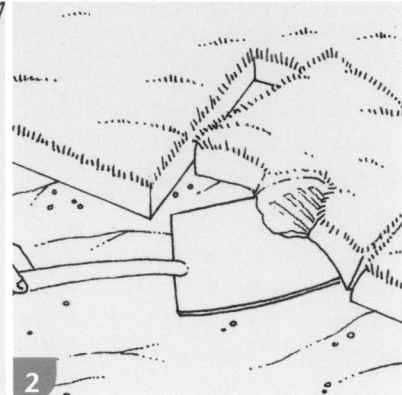

2 Gently undercut the turf with a spade and move it forward so the broken edge extends beyond the rest of the lawn.

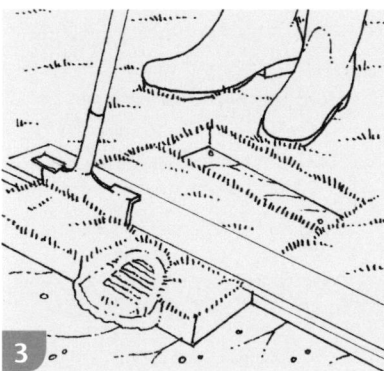

3 Place a wooden batten to line up with the rest of the lawn edge and remove the damaged turf using a half-moon cutter.

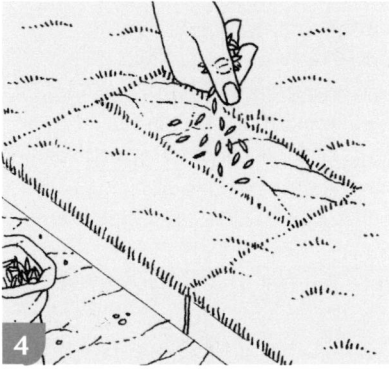

4 Fill the gap with soil, firm it, then re-seed the area with grass seed. Water well and keep off the grass so it can regrow.

do the cutting. If you have broken edges, you'll need to undertake renovation work (*see* box, above).

Using a strimmer

Electric or petrol-driven strimmers make the work of trimming edges quicker and easier. They're widely available and comparatively inexpensive. However, strimmers will never produce the neatness of

edge that hand-trimming can. If the edge has been allowed to grow long, strim first and then mow, and the mower grass box will collect up most of the bits of grass produced by the strimming. Always wear goggles when strimming and be extra careful if you are strimming near the greenhouse, conservatory or house – stones can and do fly up and may break windows.

Protecting lawn edges

Lawn edges are very vulnerable to scalping, which occurs when the grass along the extreme edge of the lawn is cut too low. What tends to happen is that when the edge of the lawn is being mown, one wheel goes into the border or the hover cushion of air is disrupted, the mower tilts over and cuts the grass much shorter than intended. One of the easiest ways to avoid scalping and other edge damage is to introduce a firm, solid border around the lawn. This makes mowing and trimming this area much quicker and easier, and does away with the need to re-cut the edge every spring.

There are various methods of edging lawns; some are short-lived while others are much more long term. A fairly permanent but costly option is to install an apron of bricks or paving slabs bedded into cement; make sure that when the edging is in place it's just below the level of the lawn so it doesn't foul the mower blades.

Ready-made lawn edgings
Most DIY stores and garden centres have a selection of ready-made lawn edgings; you can also buy them from mail-order companies and of course specialist firms on the internet. Commonly used materials include corrugated metal, rigid plastic, and bamboo or 'log' rolls.

These are all easy enough to fit yourself. Some come with spikes along their bottom edge. Alternatively, you may need to insert pegs at regular intervals and then slot the edging between the lawn edge and the pegs. Ideally, use a rubber mallet to drive the spikes or pegs into the ground so you don't damage the edging.

Decorative edgings
If you want to define the edge of your lawn in a more decorative way, you could choose from a range including miniature picket fences and willow hurdles, intricate cast-iron work or slightly cheaper black-coated steel. Many decorative edges provide only a little protection for the lawn itself, but they look pretty and can be used to prevent border plants flopping over the grass, which in itself is a good thing, as grass dislikes being shaded and smothered.

There is a wide variety of lawn edgings available to suit every style of garden. ① Chunky white gravel chips contrast with an aluminium edging strip.

② A traditional brick edge creates a tidy finish between slate chippings and lawn. ③ Old brick edging looks rustic and perfectly complements the lavender.

Don't forget
With any lawn edging, once it is fixed in place, go along the lawn side and backfill any gaps with soil – the grass will soon grow into it.

Feeding your lawn

Once planted, your grass plants depend on you to provide the balanced nutrition they need to survive and thrive. In most gardens, nutrient levels are less than ideal. Also, nutrients may be washed (leeched) through the soil by rainwater or during summer watering and so sink out of range of the roots, or other plants may compete for food. With grass, in particular, the quantity of leaf we remove with every cut means that the plants really do need regular boosts if they are to grow well.

The leaves of a plant manufacture their own food from sunlight by a process called photosynthesis. This provides the essential sugars and starches that the plant requires to live and to grow. So plants really rely on their leaves.

Lawns need spring and autumn feeds to keep them in tip-top condition. Some gardeners prefer to feed every six weeks between spring and autumn for a really lush sward.

To manufacture its food efficiently, a plant also needs minerals and trace elements from the soil, which are taken in by the roots in a watery solution. The main requirements are for nitrogen (N), phosphorus (P) and potassium (K), plus minute amounts of copper, iron, boron, magnesium, manganese, zinc and molybdenum. The correct quantity of each of these will enable the plant to thrive. Reduced amounts of any or all of them will limit the rate of growth to some degree. If the plant suffers from complete lack of any one of these nutrients, it will show distinct signs of the deficiency in its growth or leaf coloration. Similarly, if the plant has too much of one kind, this may also show in the type of growth that it makes.

The effects of mowing

Every time you reduce the leaf area of your grass plants through mowing, you partially remove the plant's ability to produce its own food; if you like a trim lawn you might do this twice, or even three times a week in summer. If you were to treat any other plant in the same way it would be unlikely to survive.

Mowing also takes its toll on the soil in which the grass is growing. In

You can scatter lawn fertilizer by hand on a dry, still day or use a distributor (*see* page 50). Wash hands well after application or wear gloves.

the normal course of events in a garden (or anywhere else that plants grow for that matter), nutrients are recycled naturally as leaves fall to the ground and gradually decay, returning any goodness they contain to the soil, which replenishes its reserves. During mowing, it is standard practice to remove the grass clippings (*see* page 56). This is to prevent a build-up of old material (thatch) that could lead to diseases taking hold; it also looks neater and avoids treading bits of grass into the house. However, it also means that the soil is being robbed of nutrients with every mowing.

Over time, the soil nutrients that a lawn needs for balanced growth will all become depleted. Nitrogen, which is responsible for growth and the greenness of the grass, becomes exhausted at a much faster rate than phosphorus and potassium, because it drains away more quickly with heavy watering. Without feeding, the grass will start to turn paler green and the growth will become thin and sparse. This gives weeds the opportunity to establish, which causes increased competition for light, water and remaining nutrients.

Redressing the balance

To have a healthy lawn, you need to feed it on a regular basis to add what you have effectively taken away with mowing. The lighter and more free-draining the soil is, the more fertilizer the lawn will need. It's vital to time the feeding so that the grass can benefit from it. Luckily, the grass fertilizer manufacturers take the guesswork out of this by giving their products names like 'Spring feed' or 'Autumn feed'. They also provide details on how to use their products – always follow their guidelines when you apply feed: too much can be as detrimental as too little, causing leaf scorching or even killing the grass.

Spring feed Spring feed tends to contain a higher level of nitrogen (N), as it promotes strong, vigorous leaf growth in the early stages by replacing what has been washed out of the soil during winter. Phosphorus (P) and potassium (K) will also be present in this feed to prevent the growth being too soft (fast growth produces more delicate leaves – think lanky), which makes it vulnerable to damage, and to encourage new root development.

Autumn feed In autumn feed, the nitrogen content is reduced so that the growth becomes harder (slower growth produces tougher leaves) and is able to withstand the winter temperatures better.

Luckily, grass responds remarkably quickly to being fed, especially if soluble fertilizers are used. The lawn becomes a rich, deep-green colour – a visible sign of its improvement in health – and the nutrients help it to build up a greater resistance to lawn pests and diseases and keep it growing more vigorously.

When to feed

It makes life easier if you can time feeding the lawn to coincide with the right weather conditions, so watch the forecast and pick your moment. Ideally, the soil should be moist when you feed the lawn, but if

the grass is dry when you apply the fertilizer you'll need rain within about 48 hours, otherwise the fertilizer may scorch the grass. If no rain is forthcoming, you'll need to water instead. Liquid and dry soluble formulations are mixed with water before application, so are less likely to produce scorching in dry weather.

How to feed

Feed is sold as a powder or in granules, which are scattered evenly on the lawn, or in a water-soluble form, which is watered in. Organic alternatives to chemical feeds are available, made from a variety of ingredients including seaweed, bonemeal, blood and fish, and these are less likely to cause scorching.

Feeding is simple but must be done with care, especially if you use a powdered or granular feed. These fertilizers are highly concentrated and if applied at the wrong rate, or spilled onto the lawn by mistake, they can kill the grass.

Before you begin, measure out the amount of fertilizer recommended for your size of lawn. Apply half of the total amount of fertilizer in one direction, then the remainder at right angles to the lines of the first. This method makes distribution much more even than if you were to apply the whole lot at once.

While you can use a bucket and scatter the granules by hand (wearing rubber gloves), to ensure

Liquid lawn feeds are great for a pick-me-up as they deliver nutrients to the grass plants very quickly. They're also the easiest and safest to use.

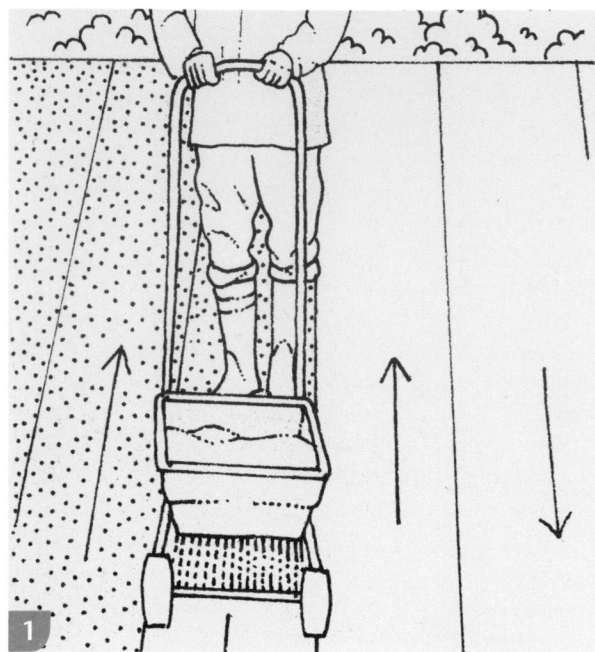

Pour half of the fertilizer you need over the base of the distributor and set the calibrator to deliver the feed at half the recommended rate. Walk up and down the length of the lawn at a steady pace. Take great care not to overlap the previous pass. Turn off the distributor when you turn at the end of each pass and turn it on again when you start the next pass.

Pour the remaining half of the fertilizer in the distributor and repeat the process shown in step 1, but this time apply the fertilizer across the width of the lawn. Again, be very careful not to overlap the previous strip of turf. After you've finished distributing the feed, clean out the distributor thoroughly. Any fertilizer left in the machine may get damp and cause corrosion.

an even application it's better to use a specially designed distributor. Even then, you need to take care not to overlap areas of lawn, as you'll see the difference when the grass starts to grow. Before you begin, wheel the distributor on a hard surface or path to avoid dumping high concentrations of fertilizer on the lawn as the application begins.

Distributors make easy work of applying lawn feeds, grass seed, weedkillers and other granular formulations. Ensure you use the recommended quantities.

Watering your lawn

For most of us, rain is an inconvenience and we're only too happy when it stops. However, our plants (including grass) need rain to survive. We might feel it's been raining for hours, and it's easy for us to think that there has been plenty to satisfy the garden, but the only real way to find out is to dig down into the soil. In summer, you may find that only the very top few inches are wet – and evaporation from the surface soon gets rid of that, leaving the lawn dry again before long.

Current concerns about water conservation mean that only new lawns should be watered during prolonged dry spells.

Why water is important

Like us, plants can't live without water: all of their functions depend upon it. Every cell within every plant is filled with a water-based solution that makes it firm and strong – a bit like a balloon filled with water – and all the systems within the plant, including those that transport nutrients around, rely on water to function. Plants even need water to provide their food, because they don't 'eat' their nutrients, they 'drink' them from the soil.

You may remember from your school biology lessons that water, which holds dissolved nutrients, moves around the plant through a continuous system called osmosis. The roots absorb water at one end and the leaves and other structures lose it at the other – like a siphon. A lack of water at the roots slows down this system and the cells

within the plant start to lose their balloon-full-of-water rigidity, which we see above the surface as wilting. At this point, watering usually leads to the recovery of the plant, although it may suffer some damage to the tips.

Extreme water shortage causes the cells to lose contact with each other and, at this stage, the plant has reached its 'permanent wilting point', beyond which it cannot recover, no matter how much water is applied. One of the problems with grass is that because it is shallow rooted it is one of the first plants to suffer in a drought. However, it is also, by nature, hugely resilient and capable of speedy recovery.

Do you need to water?

Rainfall in Britain is generally sufficient for grass to survive, but there are occasional prolonged dry periods when it may suffer. A well-grown lawn can lose up to 20 litres (4.5 gallons) of water per square metre (10¾ square feet) of surface area each week in summer through evaporation alone. If you know you live in an area of low rainfall, it makes sense to seed your lawn with a drought-tolerant mixture that will survive the hard times.

The feeder roots of grass plants tend to be concentrated in the top 10cm (4in) of soil. The heat from the sun causes evaporation at the surface and this means feeder roots are vulnerable during a dry spell, as this is the first part of the soil to dry out. You can help the grass to root deeper into the soil, where the water will be available for longer, by spiking the lawn every autumn to relieve any compaction (*see* pages 57–8).

Applying the water

In recent years, water shortages have led to hosepipe bans. This has made us all more aware of our need to conserve water, but also of a lawn's capacity for recovery even after prolonged drought. As a result, established lawns are generally left to cope in spells of drought.

Newly established lawns are the exception to the rule and should not be allowed to dry out. Check to make sure that you have a sprinkler licence and that no hosepipe ban is in force at the time you need to water. Applying water in the evening means it has time to soak in while the temperatures are lower and

A drought-stricken lawn becomes yellow and patchy. Although the grass should recover when rain returns, this type of stress may allow weeds and diseases to take hold.

evaporation is less likely. There's a fine line between applying enough water and flooding the grass, so make sure you get it right.

Sprinklers There is a vast range of sprinklers available in garden centres, including static, rotary and oscillating bar varieties. Although a sprinkler is a convenient form of watering – you can leave it on and walk away – it isn't necessarily the most efficient: it loses a lot of water when in use (especially on a windy day) and tends to wet only the upper layer of soil. This results in the grass roots staying near the surface, which won't help them during future dry spells, and a lot of the water will be lost rapidly through evaporation.

Hosepipes A hosepipe is very versatile and if you simply lie it on the lawn and set it on a trickle it will do a more efficient job than a sprinkler. You need to move it every half hour. This way, you don't need to water the whole lawn every day, because the soil is wet enough to last longer. Having water deeper in the soil encourages the roots to grow downwards with it, making them more likely to survive in the future. Remember, 2.5cm (1in) of water on the surface can penetrate to a depth of 10cm (4in) if it's allowed to soak down.

Perforated hoses Also known as seep hoses, these are similar to hosepipes but they have holes along their length (also, they're often made of a rough black material). You attach them to the tap and they leak all along their length. The great thing about them is that if they're laid on the lawn they will deliver water to a huge area without much evaporation and no waste. It's important to keep them clean as the holes can block.

Watering cans You'll probably have one already, but you need to be extremely dedicated to water anything but the tiniest of lawns this way. They do come in useful for spot-treating very dry areas.

Tips for dry spells

If you're experiencing a dry spell, there are several things you can do to help your lawn survive without watering.

■ Feed the lawn (*see* pages 48–50) and remove weeds regularly to keep the grass growing vigorously and to remove competition for the available water (*see* pages 60–1).

■ Let the grass grow longer than usual so that it shades its own roots. This reduces evaporation from the surface.

■ Leave the clippings on the lawn as a mulch to retain moisture. This will help for a few weeks, but it's not good to do this continuously (*see* page 56).

Mowing the lawn

If your garden is looking a little scruffy you can give it an immediate facelift simply by mowing the lawn. It's incredible how this relatively simple task can transform the overall look of a garden. A lawn can be mown up to 50 times a year, so the quality of the mowing will have a huge influence on the quality of the lawn you produce. Mowing encourages the grass plants to spread and anchor down into the soil, as well as making the lawn pleasant to walk on. It can also eliminate many weeds and coarser-leaved grasses.

Frequency

How often you should mow is largely determined by the weather conditions and grass type, but generally you need to take the first cut in early spring and continue until early autumn, with the occasional light trim in early winter if it's mild. If the grass, soil or both are very wet, mowing is inadvisable. The ideal is to cut little and often, which keeps the grass healthy without allowing it to get too long, and before weeds start to grow.

A petrol-driven rotary mower is ideal for small to medium-sized lawns. When you're doing the first cut of the year, raise the mower blades to avoid shocking the grass.

How close to cut

An average lawn should be mown to a height of 2.5cm (1in) in summer; leave it slightly longer (about 3cm/1½in) in very dry conditions. Top-quality lawns consisting of fine-leaved grasses can be half this height. If you've had to miss a couple of mowing sessions, perhaps if you've been on holiday, the temptation is to try to get the grass back to the correct height in one cut, but this is a big mistake – taking away such a large amount of its growth reduces its vigour. As a general rule, never remove more than one-third of the grass in any one cut. It's better to bring the grass back down to its regular cutting height by lowering the height of the cut in stages over the next two or three mowings.

Very close cutting on a regular basis – for example, mowing short once a week instead of longer twice a week – will weaken the grass and expose the soil between its stems, which will encourage weed seeds to germinate and invade bare areas.

A good mower is essential to the health and appearance of your lawn. There's such a wide range of mowers on offer that it can be difficult to decide which is the best type for you and your lawn. The principal issues to look into when you're considering buying a mower is how the machine cuts, how it's driven, the cutting width, and the cost. You also need to consider the size, shape and quality of your lawn, as well as the look you're hoping to achieve.

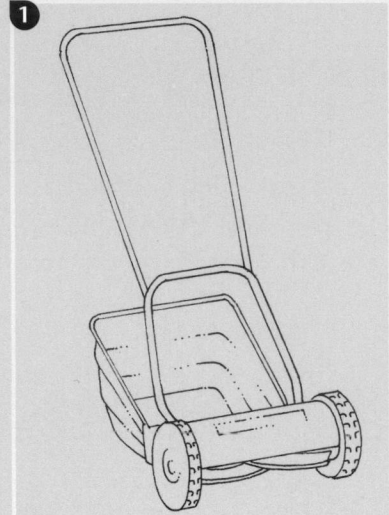

How do they cut?

There are two main types of domestic mower: cylinder and rotary. Either type can produce stripes provided they have a large rear roller.

Cylinder mowers

A cylinder mower is the best option if you desire a really first-rate lawn. It cuts in a similar way to a pair of scissors. The cylinder consists of a number of spirally arranged blades mounted on a central spindle; there is also a fixed bottom blade. As the spindle rotates, the grass is trapped between the moving and fixed blades and is cut.

Depending on the quality of the mower, the number of cutting blades on the cylinder can vary between 3 and 12: the greater the number of blades, the more even the finished cut.

Most cylinder mowers have two rollers fitted to them: a larger rear roller and a smaller front roller. The rear roller often turns the cutting cylinder. The front roller, which is in front of the cutting cylinder, supports the front of the mower and allows adjustment to the cutting height.

Most cylinder mowers come with a removable grass box for collecting the cut grass. This is usually on the front of the machine; the rotating action of the blades throws the cuttings into the box.

Rotary mowers

A rotary mower cuts with a slicing action. The knife-like blades rotate horizontally at very high speeds and cut through the grass blades on impact. The number of blades varies depending on the manufacturer but is usually two or four. The blades are made of hardened steel and must be kept very sharp or they'll damage the grass by tearing rather than cutting it.

The type of finish produced by a rotary mower is not quite as fine as that produced by a cylinder mower with more than six blades, but it is certainly on a similar level to many four- and six-bladed cylinder mowers. Rotary mowers are particularly useful for rough areas, such as orchards and verges, where the finish is not critical. They're also the best option if you're going to leave your grass to grow long occasionally or if the lawn is bumpy.

Smaller rotary mowers do not pick up clippings; larger ones have a grass box at the back (*see* centre right).

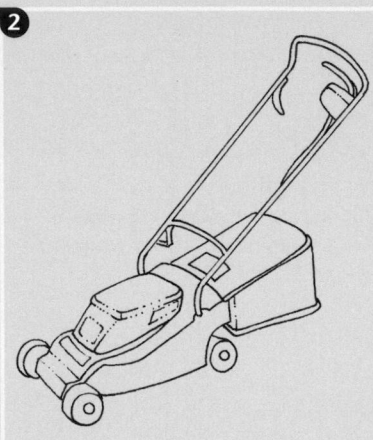

There are many factors to consider when buying a lawn mower, so choose one to suit your needs (*see* box, opposite) .
① A manual cylinder mower is suited to small lawns and gives a good finish.
② An electric rotary mower with a grass box attached to the rear is perfect for small to medium lawns.
③ Ideal for smaller lawns and difficult areas, a hover mower is light and easy to use, lift and store.

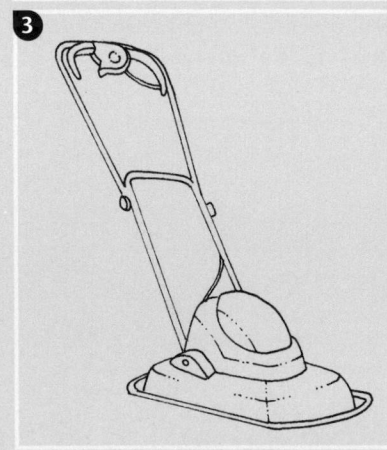

One very common variation of the rotary mower is the hover mower (*see* opposite, below). Although its cutting action is no different from other rotary mowers, this machine rides on a cushion of air and so it doesn't need wheels. When the machine is running, it produces a jet of air that is forced downwards and builds up pressure that lifts the mower off the ground. This air cushion and lack of wheels makes hover mowers very manoeuvrable, ideal for slopes, banks or uneven areas and for cutting long or wet grass.

How are they driven?
There are four methods of propulsion for mowers: hand-pushed, petrol- or diesel-operated, and those powered by mains electricity or battery.

Hand-driven mowers
Manual mowers (*see* opposite, top) rely on manpower to make them move and cut. If you keep your lawn well tended and it's not a huge area, pushing a mower doesn't have to be hard work. Hand mowers, which are always cylinder cutters, are excellent for awkward corners and restricted areas. They are quiet, too!

Petrol or diesel engines
Most walk-behind models run on petrol; ride-ons can be diesel. With cheaper walk-behind models, the blades are power driven and you have to push them along; with more costly models, the wheels are powered too. Cylinders, rotaries and hovers are all available (ride-ons tend to be rotary; cylinder versions are more pricey). For most lawns, except luxury lawns, a rotary mower is best in this category (*see* page 53).

Electric mowers
Mains-driven mowers are available in cylinder and rotary (including hover mower) designs (*see* opposite, centre and below). Again, you do the moving work while they do the cutting. They're reasonably quiet and efficient, and often lightweight. However, their big disadvantage is the power cord, which must be kept safely out of the way and will stretch only a certain distance. Don't choose electricity if you have a large lawn with a complicated shape. Generally, mains-electricity mowers are less expensive but less powerful than petrol- or diesel-driven ones.

Some mowers use a rechargeable battery to run a motor, making them the heaviest of the mowers. All battery-operated mowers are cylinder cutters.

Don't forget
If you have a big, rectangular or square lawn, choose the largest, widest lawn mower you can manoeuvre, store and afford, since it will make the job considerably quicker. If you have a smaller, more complicated lawn including narrow, awkward areas, it's more important to opt for a model with narrower cutting blades, as it will be easier to handle.

Which type of mower?

	MANUAL CYLINDER MOWER	ELECTRIC CYLINDER MOWER	PETROL CYLINDER MOWER	ELECTRIC ROTARY OR HOVER MOWER	PETROL ROTARY MOWER	PETROL OR DIESEL RIDE-ON ROTARY MOWER
Small lawns	■	■		■		
Large lawns			■		■	■
First-rate finish	■	■	■			
Overgrown grass				■	■	■
Bumpy lawn				■	■	
Awkward corners	■			■		
Speed			■	■	■	■
Light to handle	■	■		■		
Easy to maintain	■					
Relatively quiet	■	■		■		
Relatively inexpensive	■			■		
Comparatively powerful					■	■

Make sure you empty the grass out of the mower regularly; rather like a full hoover bag, a full grass box impairs the mower's ability to pick up lawn clippings.

The perfect striped lawn

Are you aiming for stripes? If so, you'll only get a striped lawn with a mower that has a roller fitted to it, as it's the angle at which the grass has been bent over that makes the stripes look a different colour.

To ensure you get an evenly striped rectangular or square lawn, start by mowing a strip along two opposite ends, then, starting at one of the other edges, mow up and down, turning the mower in your previously mown strips at each end. With a lawn that has an irregular shape, mow all around the edge to begin with. Next, mow your first row right through the centre, then mow up and down out to one side. Return to the centre and mow up and down out to the other side.

How to mow

For best results, mow around the entire edge of the lawn, then mow up and down methodically to cut all the grass evenly. If you've a petrol mower, fill it with fuel and oil on a hard surface, not on the lawn – spillages will cause brown spots. If you have an electric mower with a cable attached, start near the power point and mow away from it, as this keeps the cable away from where you're cutting and it's gradually drawn out as you work across the lawn. Always use a circuit breaker or an RCD (Residual Current Device) when working with electricity – it really isn't worth taking any risks.

Removing the grass

Ideally, grass clippings should be removed from the surface of the lawn, either by collecting them in a grass box attached to the mower or by raking them from the lawn for composting. Although it makes good sense to leave clippings on the lawn when the weather is very hot and dry, to reduce moisture loss, generally it isn't advisable.

There are two main reasons for not leaving clippings. First, if clippings are allowed to accumulate they form a layer of dead or rotting grass called thatch. The new grass will tend to root into this layer rather than the soil below, which makes the lawn susceptible to drying out in summer and waterlogging in winter. Fungal infection is also much more likely where the thatch has built up, because there is less airflow at soil level (*see* pages 63–4).

The second reason is that clippings encourage worm activity. While this is welcome in flower beds, it's not the case on a lawn. The worms will try to draw the dead and dying grass clippings down into the soil, leaving worm casts on the surface (*see* page 62). These little mounds of soil are not only unsightly but they can be destructive – you'll need to brush them to flatten them out before mowing the lawn, otherwise the soil causes excessive wear and tear on the mower's cutting blades. Also, since the casts are made up of soil from below the lawn they often contain weed seeds.

Scarifying, aerating and top-dressing

Once the lawn is growing well, you need to undertake routine maintenance to keep it looking its best. As well as mowing the grass regularly to keep it neat, and weeding and feeding regularly, you should maintain good hygiene by removing any dead material that accumulates and making sure the lawn drains well. For these tasks you'll need a garden fork and spade, a spring-tine and garden rake, a hollow-tined aerator and a stiff broom.

Scarifying the lawn using a spring-tine or fan rake to remove moss and thatch is a satisfying and energetic job; you'll be amazed at how much material you gather in a single session.

Scarifying

The process of scarifying improves the overall health of the lawn and is best carried out once a year. It involves deep raking of the lawn's surface, which allows air to get to the grass roots and at the same time prunes the roots. This encourages a much more finely branched root system, which in turn improves the grass's ability to absorb nutrients and water. It also removes thatch (dead and decaying grass) and moss from the lawn's surface.

On a larger lawn, it's considerably quicker to use a mechanical scarifier, available in tool-hire shops. They have rotating, knife-like blades that rip out the thatch.

How and when to scarify

Scarifying is simple: just tug a rake (preferably a spring-tine rake) through the lawn so that the tines repeatedly pull at the tangled mass of grass. If there is thatch and moss on the surface, work across the lawn in one direction and then rake a second time at 90 degrees to the first raking. After scarifying, remove and dispose of all the debris from the lawn's surface.

Scarifying is best done in early autumn, about two weeks after treatment for moss (see pages 60–1). Don't do it before killing moss, or you'll simply spread moss further around your lawn. You may be able to combine scarifying with collecting up autumn leaves. Alternatively, you could combine it with mowing in late summer, when it can be a good way of weakening weeds spreading through the lawn by means of long, trailing shoots. The raking draws up these shoots and mowing soon afterwards cuts them off.

In late spring or early summer, you can spot-scarify to remove patches of dead moss. It's important not to scarify the whole lawn at this time of the year though, or you risk setting it back for the whole summer.

Aerating

Unless they're regularly aerated, most lawns will eventually begin to suffer from compaction (see page 34) as the soil settles and becomes denser, and any air trapped between the soil particles is driven out. Without air, the grass roots are unable to function efficiently.

probably not worth doing the whole area – just choose the places where you know the children play, or where you stand to hang up the washing, or where you've seen water lying for any length of time. To aerate a lawn, drive a garden fork into the soil in compacted areas so that the tines penetrate to a depth of 7cm (3in).

There are also several specialist pieces of equipment available that help with aeration. A hollow-tined aerator (see page 35) consists of a set of hollow, finger-like spikes that you push into the soil at intervals of 15–20cm (6–8in) and to a depth of about 15cm (6in). A plug or core of soil from the lawn is squeezed up into the hollow tine, leaving a small, narrow hole in the ground. The next time you insert the hollow-tined aerator into the ground, this plug is expelled onto the lawn surface. Once an area has been treated, collect up the cores, which can be stacked to make compost. Hollow-tining is the most effective form of aeration and needs doing only every three years or so in areas of heavy compaction.

Slitters and solid-tine aerators are also available. The slitter cuts narrow slits and its blades also do some pruning of the grass roots as they're pushed into the soil. Mechanical aerators make life a lot easier if you have a large area to do and they are available from tool-hire shops.

Make small, deep holes in your lawn using a garden fork to improve air supply to the grass roots, increase drainage and ease compaction.

Although we can't see what's happening underground, the growth above ground will provide some clues. The grass will be stunted, with fewer new leaves forming so that the lawn looks sparse, and the grass may start to turn a pale greenish yellow rather than being a healthy dark green.

Aerating a lawn is simply a method of getting air back down to the root zone in the soil so that the roots can breathe and the lawn can grow again. The most effective way to do this is by creating deep, narrow holes in the lawn. These enable air to get deeper down into the soil and they can greatly improve drainage. Regular attention to drainage is particularly important for lawns on heavier soils, which are much more prone to compaction than lighter, sandy soils.

How and when to aerate

Basic aeration or spiking is best done once a year in early autumn, after scarification. It's quite tiring work, and compaction is unlikely to be bad throughout your lawn, so it's

Pricking

Pricking is when only the top 2.5cm (1in) or so of soil is penetrated. It is done with a slitter or solid-tine aerator in spring or summer to ensure that food and water can get into the soil near the grass roots, where it's needed.

Applying top-dressing

The last piece of the annual lawn-care jigsaw puzzle is to apply a top-dressing in autumn, after scarifying and aerating. This task is often bypassed altogether, which is a pity as top-dressing is very beneficial for the lawn, particularly on heavier soils such as clay. The benefits are that it fills holes and hollows so scalping (*see* page 47) is avoided, and it encourages the grass to produce new roots and runners. It can also improve drainage and moisture retention. When a sandy top-dressing mixture is used on heavy soil, it improves drainage, and when a loamy mix is used on light soil, it improves the lawn's water-retaining potential.

Top-dressing a lawn involves covering it with a thin layer of good-quality topsoil, or sand and some organic material, such as peat-substitute. (Don't confuse lawn top-dressing with border top-dressing, where fertilizer is sprinkled around plants.) The layer should be thin enough for you to be able to see the blades of grass poking through it. If it's any thicker, you'll smother the grass. If you want to add more than 1.5cm (½in) – say in a deep hollow – apply it in two stages with a two- to three-week interval between the first and second application, to avoid weakening the grass.

Put the finishing touches to your autumn lawn-maintenance routine by filling shallow dips with a top-dressing. The grass will soon grow back through.

Coping with weeds and moss

Newly sown lawns are much more likely to have weeds than those recently made from good-quality turf, and old, neglected lawns are likely to consist of weeds and moss more than anything else. The methods of dealing with these problems are the same for all lawns – barring those that have gone beyond all hope and must be renewed.

To get rid of weeds you must either dig them up by hand or use a suitable weedkiller. To get rid of moss you must use a moss killer and/or scarify the lawn (*see* page 57). You must then promise yourself to be more diligent about caring for your lawn so that the weeds don't dare to show their faces again! Seriously, all lawns grow weeds from

Self-heal and white clover are threatening to take over this patch of lawn; both are difficult to eradicate even with chemicals.

Almost every lawn has its resident daisy plants, but this is a comparatively easy weed to keep under control and can be dug out by hand or killed with a weedkiller.

time to time; the seeds are always present in the soil, waiting for the opportunity to emerge, and then there's the generosity of passing birds in making their deposits, and the light waft of a breeze bringing pretty dandelion parachutes gently to rest on your precious sward.

Organic remedies

If you prefer to garden organically, it's particularly important to look after your lawn well and tend to its every need on a regular basis. This way, you'll encourage healthy growth without the use of chemical assistance. The idea is that if your grass is growing vigorously there will not be sufficient space for the weeds to take hold.

If you're not using chemicals you'll need to dig out any weeds that appear by hand, or live with the less invasive types. The soil of a newly

sown lawn is comparatively loose and it's easy to dig up annual weeds before they get a hold. Make a small hole and refill it with soil, firming the turf around it after you've removed the weeds. Regular mowing will keep the taller weeds down, but unfortunately it can't eradicate the lower-growing, rosette-forming types such as daisies, plantains and dandelions, known as broad-leaved weeds. If you want a perfect lawn you may have to resort to a chemical weedkiller to get rid of these.

Chemical treatments

When it comes to chemical weedkillers, you can either spot-treat individual weeds or use a broadcast weed-and-feed treatment, which you sprinkle over the whole lawn. It's a good idea to feed at the same time as weeding, to encourage the grass to grow and fill the gaps before weeds are allowed to take over again.

Weed-and-feed combinations have been found to be more effective than straight weedkiller, but if you need to treat a large area that is mostly weeds, use a weedkiller that doesn't contain fertilizer or you'll only encourage them further. Where large bare patches appear after weeds are killed off, re-seed with grass after about six weeks (*see* page 65).

All types of weedkiller tend to contain similar active ingredients in differing quantities. Any chemical weedkillers that kill coarse grasses will also kill your lawn grasses, so rather than using weedkiller for these, cut through their clumps with a half-moon cutter or spade just before mowing and mow regularly.

Lawn sand This will deal with moss as well as weeds and also acts as a fertilizer. It is fine sand that contains ammonium sulphate and iron sulphate. When applied to a lawn, it settles on the wider surface area of weed leaves and moss and the iron sulphate destroys them by scorching. Narrow grass leaves are not affected – they may temporarily go black but will soon recover. When it lands on the soil, the ammonium sulphate in the lawn sand gives the grass a boost.

Use lawn sand on a sunny day from late spring to early summer. It can be applied in the same way as granular or powdered feeds (*see* pages 48–50). If rain doesn't fall within a couple of days, give the whole lawn a good watering. Don't

Liquid weedkillers are ideal for treating small patches of weeds. Use them on a dry, still day so there is no risk of spray damaging the plants in your borders.

mow for at least three or four days and don't use the first lot of clippings as a mulch around plants.

Granular or powder weed/moss killers These formulations kill selected weeds and are mostly combined with fertilizers. They are applied in the same way as granular or powdered feeds (*see* pages 48–50). Like lawn sand, use them on a sunny day from late spring to early summer, water after two days if there has been no rain and don't mow the lawn for about three or four days after application to enable the chemicals to work. A lawn must be at least a year old before it can withstand these chemicals.

For just the odd interloper, spray-on spot weedkillers are the best choice rather than treating the whole lawn. The ready-mixed versions are pricey, but you're paying for convenience.

Liquid weedkillers These are applied directly onto broad-leaved weeds via a watering can or sprayer in spring or early summer. Use the product according to the instructions and clean out your watering can or sprayer well after use.

Spot weedkillers Perfect for treating individual weeds in the grass as and when you need to, you usually spray spot weedkillers on the offending weeds or paint them on. Several applications may be needed, so they're really only suitable for the odd weed, not large areas.

Other lawn problems

Despite your best efforts, you may find that your lawn falls prey to pests and diseases or develops worn patches or lumps and bumps. Wear and tear can happen at any time and new lawns will settle a little, especially in the first few years, leaving unexpected unevenness. Fortunately, if you've made your lawn, you will have all the necessary skills to deal with most of these problems, and the majority are easy to overcome.

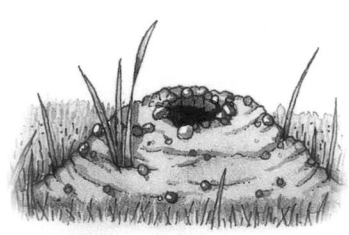

Piles of earth

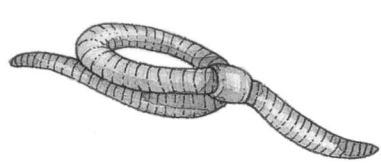

Earthworms

These creatures, which are so useful elsewhere in the garden, are unwelcome on a lawn as their activities result in worm casts. These are small coils of sticky soil on the surface (*see* below) and are particularly evident in spring and autumn. (Just in case you're wondering, surface-casting worms, which leave worm casts, are not particularly good aerators of soil.)

Worm casts contain weed seeds and provide the perfect growing medium for them. If you have a few worm casts on your lawn, sweep them into the sward with a garden broom before mowing; if they're present in abundance, consider increasing the acidity of the soil by using lawn sand (*see* page 61).

Ants

Ant hills (*see* below) are less harmful than worm casts, because they're dry and appear only in summer, when the ants nest. The solution is the same as for worm casts – sweep the earth away before mowing. If the ants become a real nuisance, locate the nest and dig it up to expose the eggs.

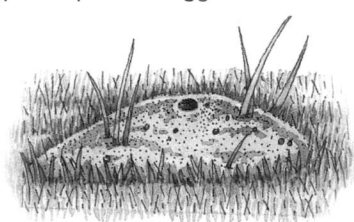

Mining bees

These bees, which do not sting, produce tiny, conical, volcano-type mounds of soil on the lawn surface (*see* top right). These resemble ant hills (*see* above) but they have a more distinct 'crater' at the top. The mounds are a result of the bees nesting under lawns and paths; in the process of making their

nests, they bring soil to the surface. Like ant hills, these mounds are not a serious problem – they're just an aesthetic nuisance, and you need to disperse the earth using a broom before you mow.

Moles

These little black, furry creatures do dreadful damage to lawns, sometimes almost overnight, leaving large piles of earth on the lawn (*see* below). If you have fertile soil that is a haven to earthworms, the moles will consider themselves to be in paradise: they'll make themselves at home and won't leave voluntarily. The only permanent solutions for dealing with moles are trapping or poison, neither of which are pleasant and both of which are best left to the professionals.

Yellow patches

Leatherjackets

The most harmful of all lawn pests, leatherjackets are the larvae of crane flies or daddy-long-legs. The eggs are laid in late summer and the grubs hatch in autumn. They soon get hungry and their favourite food is the roots of your grass. You'll notice the lawn going yellow in patches (*see* below), particularly in spring, and bird activity may draw your attention to certain areas. If you suspect that they may be present, water a patch of lawn and cover it overnight with a piece of black plastic – the blighters will be on the surface of the lawn in the morning and you can leave them for the starlings to feast on. Where the problem is localized, you might decide to live with it – pamper your

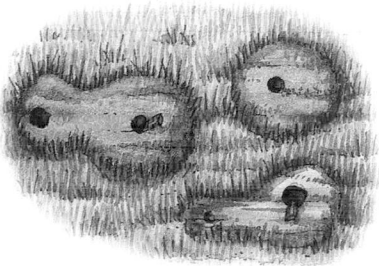

lawn to enable it to resist all but the worst attacks. Poorly drained lawns are particularly susceptible to these creatures. Biological controls (*see* page 64) will reduce your overall leatherjacket population.

Chafer grubs

The harm caused by the small, C-shaped chafer grub (*see* below) is similar to leatherjacket damage, but chafer grubs are less widespread. Luckily, the biological controls that deal with leatherjackets (*see* page 64) will also see off chafers.

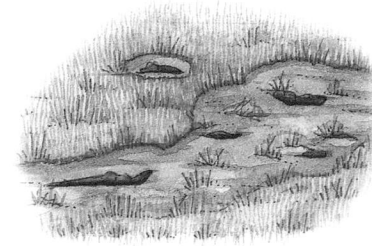

Fusarium patch

This fungus produces yellow-brown circles on the grass in autumn or winter (*see* below). These can grow a white or pinkish webby mould – cover a patch overnight with black plastic sheeting and if it is fusarium then the mould will grow. Like all fungi, fusarium needs the

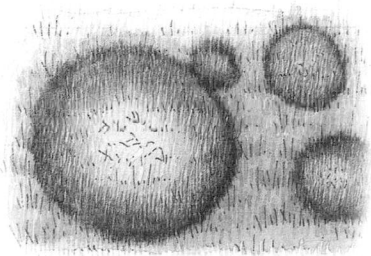

correct conditions to grow and the patches usually disappear when the weather changes. If you have problems with this fungus, you need to improve your lawn-care routine.

Dollar spot

Dollar spot is a problem in fine-leaved turf. Symptoms include disfigured grass and round yellow patches in the lawn

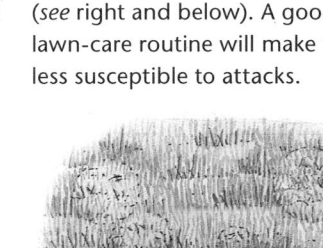

(*see* right and below). A good lawn-care routine will make the grass less susceptible to attacks.

Ophiobolus patch This rare disease kills bent grasses (hence its alternative name, bent grass take-all), and leaves sunken areas of dead grass in which weeds start to grow. It can be deterred by using lawn sand in spring and carrying out good lawn-care routines.

Bitches' urine When a female dog pees on the lawn the grass gets an overdose of nitrogen, which scorches the turf, leaving brown, circular patches surrounded by a ring of healthy, green grass. To prevent this problem, you'll have to train your bitch to urinate somewhere else. Alternatively, if it's too late for that, you'll have to follow her around with a watering can, watering the affected areas copiously to dilute the nitrogen.

Red thread

This is a problem that is confined mostly to the 'posh' end of the lawn market – the fine-leaved grasses, which need plenty of cosseting to keep them in good health in any case. Also called corticium disease, red thread is a fungal infection that turns the grass pale then pinkish. It generally occurs on a starved lawn during late summer or autumn: the first thing

you notice will be irregular patches of very pale grass. On a damp day, a close inspection will reveal very fine and thin red fungal growths among the grass blades. Red thread does not actually kill the grass, but it is very unsightly. Diligent lawn care is a good preventive measure.

Odd growths

Algae You may see a coating of black or green slime on the grass (*see* below), particularly on waterlogged or sparsely grassed lawns. You can treat algae with moss killer, but it will return unless you aerate and top-dress the soil.

Lichen Leaf-like growths (*see* below) that are dark when wet and grey and curled up when dry may appear on neglected lawns. Lawn sand can be used to get rid of the growths, but they will return without a good lawn-care routine.

Mushrooms and fairy rings

Almost any lawn will grow some tiny mushrooms or toadstools from time to time.

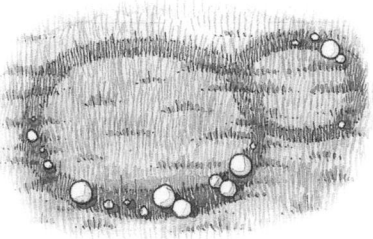

These are easily removed and won't cause any long-term problems. However, fairy rings (*see* above) vary from being a minor problem to being an eyesore. They produce a circle of greener grass that sprouts mushrooms when conditions are suitable. The only sensible solution for the average gardener is to keep the rest of the lawn well fed so the greenness of the ring is not so obvious. If you really want to be rid of them, you could remove all the affected turf and topsoil – down to a depth of 30cm (12in) and 30cm (12in) beyond the ring's boundary – and replace it. However, this seems a fairly extreme move and sometimes it makes sense just to live with a few imperfections.

Biological controls

Some of the insects that we consider pests can be controlled by means of tiny creatures called nematodes (microscopic eelworms). The nematodes attack the insects in various ways, including laying eggs inside them or using them as a meal. Scientists have devised ways to produce these nematodes under controlled conditions, which means we can buy them to do a bit of guerrilla work on our behalf when needed. There are biological controls for vine weevils, slugs, red spider mites, leatherjackets and chafer grubs. The one for leatherjackets and chafer grubs is called *Steinernema feltiae* and can be applied to lawns in autumn and spring. It is an effective remedy and is harmless to the environment, but it isn't cheap.

Bumps and hollows

Both bumps and hollows can result in scalping of the surrounding lawn (see page 47). Shallow indentations can be dealt with by top-dressing (see page 59), but deeper ones and bumps need more vigorous attention (see below). Always deal with bumps in this way – trying to push them down with a spade won't work. If you have suckers in the lawn, dig them out using this method rather than simply wrenching them out.

Bare patches

If you know what caused the bare patch, deal with this first. For example, if it was a spillage of oil dig out all the contaminated soil and replace it with clean topsoil.

To re-seed, prick the area with a garden fork, rake the surface to form a seed bed (see page 38) and then sow seed thinly and water. Protect the area from birds and other bypassers until the seed has germinated and is growing strongly.

To re-turf, remove the dead patch leaving a square or rectangular shape. Dig lightly over the exposed soil surface and water well. Lay the new turves over the area, cutting them to fit as closely as possible. Firm them down and fill any gaps with fine sand. Water them in, too.

Keep newly sown areas of grass protected with netting or loose-weave hessian until the new grass appears.

HOW TO correct bumps and hollows

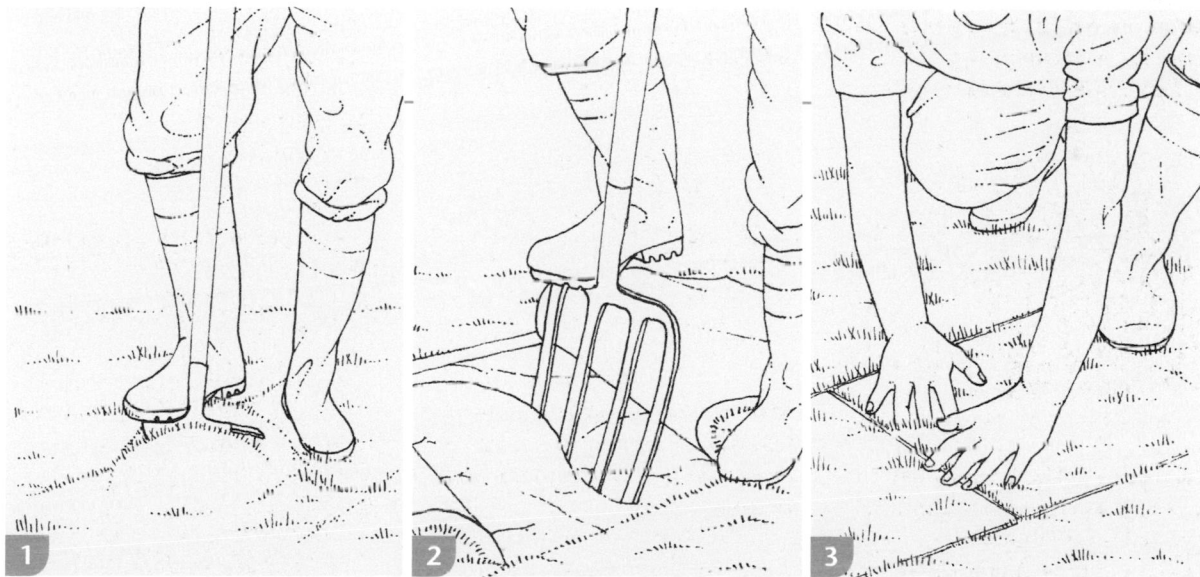

1 Using a half-moon edger, cut an H-shape around and across the bumpy or hollow area. Undercut the turf with a spade and carefully peel it back on either side.

2 Remove the bump or fill the hollow with extra soil, as necessary, until the area is level. Don't expose subsoil, or if you do, carefully reserve the topsoil, dig out some subsoil and put the topsoil back down.

3 When the ground is completely level, roll down the cut edges into their previous position. Fill the incisions by pushing sifted soil between the cracks, then water the whole area thoroughly.

Hard surfaces

Landscaping materials such as bricks, paving, gravel and wood – and the way you use them in your garden – are a major factor in its success. A well-devised deck or patio may mean the difference between you being encouraged to slip out and enjoy your outdoor space when you have a moment or lingering indoors because you can't bear to skate across an algae-ridden deck or rock across a patio whose paving stones are lifting. Whether you're planning a new area or improving an existing one, have a good look at the vast range of materials on offer – they should provide plenty of inspiration.

Considering the options

If you're installing new hard landscaping and have been through the process of deciding where you want to put paths and patios, as described in the designing section of the book (*see* pages 18–27), the next step is choosing the materials. By now, you'll probably have begun to think about what you want, but while it's fun to give free rein to your imagination, there are practicalities you need to take into consideration.

Cost

Whether we like it or not, for most of us cost is an overriding factor in our choice of any product. The price of surfacing varies from being pretty reasonable to extremely expensive, so before you set your heart on finest marble paving from Italy, find out how much it costs. Do some research: local stone may be cheaper than materials that have travelled a considerable distance, although this isn't always the case. Price is less of an issue if the area is quite small, such as a short path, but it can get out of hand if you're planning a large area of paving. Set yourself a sensible budget for the whole project and try to stay within it – it's no good having the patio of your dreams if you can no longer afford to live in the house.

Availability

Availability and timing are also important considerations. Some suppliers may have minimum orders below which it isn't financially viable

A brick path leads to a secluded seat in the corner of a garden. The worn bricks are warm in colour and blend well with the old stone wall.

for them to go. At the other end of the scale, some merchants may be unable to get hold of large quantities immediately and may have to deliver your order in smaller, staggered batches. Check that the supplier will definitely have enough of your chosen material – you really don't want to run out halfway through. Ideally, buy materials from the same batch or you may find variation in colour. When working out how many paving slabs or bricks you're going to need, factor in breakages. If you're going to be doing a lot of cutting to size, add five per cent on top of the total figure to allow for this.

In this town garden, the black painted deck, dark slate chippings and the sharp lines of black marble furniture are softened by sympathetic planting, making a smart, contemporary space.

A curving wall shelters the seating area in this modern show garden. The natural travertine paving enhances the smooth lime render of the wall.

DIY or contractor?

If you want to do the work yourself, be honest about your fitness, level of competence and time you have to devote to the task. The last thing you want is to start the patio in spring only to have regrets and then spend the summer in what looks like a muddy building site rather than enjoying your outdoor area. If you have any doubts, why not get some quotes from contractors? Although it will almost certainly be more costly and possibly less satisfying than doing the work yourself, a good contractor will have all the tools necessary for the task and the

Disguising manhole covers

If there is a manhole cover (or inspection hatch) where you want your path or patio, you don't have to compromise your design. There are covers available that have a lip around the edge, forming a tray-like surface. You simply fill this tray with your choice of hard surfacing, matching its layout to the rest of the patio or path. On a lawn, such trays can also be filled with turf, to minimize the impact of an inspection hatch, although you will need to water carefully to ensure the grass stays alive.

Who would guess that concealed beneath this striking, ammonite-encrusted, removable paving stone is a manhole?

Suitability

It doesn't matter how much you like a surface, if it doesn't go with the surroundings, it will never look as good as it would in the right place. For example, you might fall in love with terracotta tile flooring on a holiday visit to a beautiful house in the Mediterranean, but before you rush out and pave your patio with it, be realistic. Will it look as good in your back garden on a wet, windy winter's day? Maybe not. Often, using locally sourced materials works best from this point of view as they blend in with your house and other structures in the area.

Although it's often sensible to opt for a simple design, that doesn't stop you from creating interesting shapes. Many manufacturers produce sets of paving in circles, hexagons or even stars, with decorative inserts and detailing. By buying the set, you can have, say, a circular pattern (to complement a round table) within a square shape without any difficult cutting. This is a really easy way to achieve a great result. Decking (*see* pages 91–7) can also be bought as an entire kit, including steps, pergolas, balustrades, and so on, which keeps calculating costs as well as its construction simple.

experience to do it quickly and well. If a lot of excavation work is needed – for example, in order to level a sloping area for a patio – it makes good sense to use a contractor, since it will require a lot of hard labour and earth-moving equipment.

Fine-tuning your plans

You should already have a good idea of the overall shape of your patio or path (*see* pages 26–7). Make sure that this shape influences your choice of material – that way, you can save yourself, or a contractor, a lot of cutting and fitting of large paving stones into small spaces.

Looking at your garden from above often reveals the best spot for the patio and suitable routes for paths through the area.

A complex series of levels disguises the fact that this garden is built in a restricted area. The deck merges gently with the patio, which looks spacious and secluded.

If you're creating a patio, choose the spot for your table and chairs and make sure the surface is level there. Plan the route you'll take to and from the house and consider installing lighting – at ground level or above. Think about practicalities such as cleaning: a rough surface will attract more dirt than a smooth one – how easy will it be to sweep? Safety may be an issue, particularly for children or old people – do you need steps with a handrail? Will you need a balustrade? Consider wear and tear – if it's a path that you'll regularly use for moving the lawn mower or wheeling a wheelbarrow, don't pick materials that can't stand up to the traffic. It's always worth asking builders' merchants or paving suppliers for practical advice.

Paving, path and decking materials

When choosing materials for a path or patio your ultimate choice has to be fit for purpose, suit the surroundings and look good. It must also be practical to install and maintain. Below are just some of the materials available, and their advantages and disadvantages.

Bricks

These are great for creating a path or smaller area of paving and they can be laid in any pattern you like. Old bricks need cleaning to remove any mortar and then laying onto a firm base. For paving, it's advisable to use special engineering bricks, which withstand frost and wet conditions better than wall bricks. Reclaimed bricks look particularly good in gardens of older houses or cottage gardens. For larger areas, consider using concrete paving made to look like bricks – it's quicker and easier to lay. (*See also* pages 75–81.)

Natural stone

Stone can be expensive, but it looks wonderful in the right setting, and it often has colour variations within it that make it even more attractive. Granite, sandstone, fired clay and slate can all be used for paving. Local reclaimed stone is often more fitting than imported materials as well as more environmentally sound. It can be tricky to lay as it's heavy and the pieces are often irregular. (*See also* page 80.)

Concrete

Poured concrete is relatively easy to lay and inexpensive. It will last for many years without any real maintenance apart from cleaning. It can be very plain to look at but there are many ways of making it more interesting by using concrete paints and creating textured surfaces. The disadvantage is that it can be very difficult (and heavy) to remove. (*See also* pages 85–6.)

Concrete paving slabs come in lots of shapes, sizes and colours and you can arrange them into many patterns. Quality and price vary considerably – if it's for a utility area, low-price paving is perfectly adequate, but you may prefer something more attractive and costly for the patio. Paving and blocks are fairly easy to lay, hardwearing and need little maintenance, apart from cleaning. (*See also* pages 75–7.)

Wood

Wood can be cut to fit any area. It's very portable and easy to work with, and there's lots of choice to suit different tastes and budgets. It can be painted or stained any colour you like and will last many years, provided you remove any algae or fungi that begin to colonize it and treat it every year against the weather. Decking can be bought in kit form or custom made. (*See also* pages 91–7.)

Gravel and other loose materials

Loose materials such as gravel, bark, slate chippings, ornamental pebbles and cobbles come in various shapes, sizes and colours. They're perfect for awkward areas and are extremely easy to lay, producing results in minutes. However, loose materials don't provide a very good base for furniture: you may find your chair sinking if you use them as the base in the seating area. Many loose materials need topping up from time to time, especially bark, which will rot down within a few years. (*See also* pages 87–90.)

The range of hard surfaces is vast. Many materials can be combined to create a blend of colours, shapes and textures.
① A row of regular, rectangular bricks radiates out from a circular arrangement of cobbles in this courtyard.
② An intense area of deep-blue slate chippings forms a striking contrast with its edging of white stone.
③ The beauty of wood lies in its soft, warm appearance and clean, straight lines.

Tools and equipment

The following tools and equipment will come in useful if you're planning to build your own patio or path or if you're installing decking. Some items of equipment are fairly basic and you're likely to have them in your tool kit; others are a lot more specialized, in which case it might be worth hiring them from a tool-hire shop rather than buying them.

Preparing the site

The following items are needed to excavate the site and lay the foundations for hard surfacing (*see* pages 72–4).

Hammer drill Useful if you need to dig up old, unwanted paving or concrete before you begin (available from tool hire shops).

Measuring tape Choose one that is at least 10m (33ft) long for measuring the site.

Wooden pegs, mallet, string All these enable you to mark out the site and adjust the levels to ensure that you end up with a flat surface.

Builder's square To ensure that corners of the proposed patio or path are completely square.

Spade, shovel and wheelbarrow Essential for digging the site and transporting the surplus rubble away. For large areas, you may want to hire a mini-digger and a skip.

Plate compactor or whacker For tamping down and compacting base layers such as soil and foundation material (*see* right).

Wooden plank and spirit level These are both vital for ensuring the site is level. The plank needs to be about 2m (6ft) long and must be completely straight.

Wood offcut Needed when making a 'fall' in a patio to ensure surface water runs away from the house and into the garden or a drain.

Laying the surface

These items are needed for pouring concrete (*see* pages 85–6), laying paving (*see* pages 75–81) or installing decking (*see* pages 91–7).

Concrete mixer Useful for mixing large amounts of concrete.

Wooden boards, hammer and nails Needed for making shuttering or the formwork that keeps poured concrete in bounds.

Plastic sheet A weighted waterproof covering is useful for protecting areas of wet concrete.

Club hammer and bolster chisel For cutting paving stones and bricks. Alternatively, you could hire a stone splitter.

Mixing board and bucket You can buy special boards for mixing concrete and mortar on, or use an old flat board that you may already have in your shed. A bucket is useful for larger quantities.

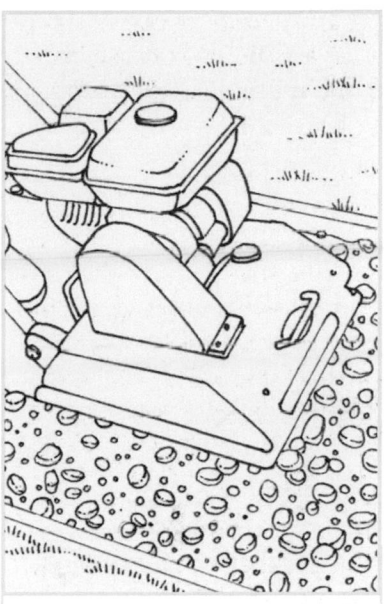

Plate compactors are readily available at tool-hire shops and make light work of levelling and compacting the foundations of paths and patios.

Bricklayer's trowel For applying mortar for paving and bricks.

Raking tool or pointing trowel Either of these will help you to make neat joints between the paving slabs or brickwork. Alternatively, you could use a stick or similar pointed object.

Brush Use a brush to sweep surplus grouting mix off the surface of paving slabs to prevent staining.

Basic tool kit Essential for installing decking. Includes drill and drill bits, spanner, screwdriver, saw and hammer, as well as galvanized coach bolts, joist hangers, nails and/or screws and a nail gun to make the job quicker and easier.

Preparing the site for hard surfacing

Whatever type of hard surface you choose – paving slabs, brick, natural stone, gravel or poured concrete – the initial work required to prepare the site is very similar. For a long-lasting, good-looking end result, you need to make strong foundations. As with many other DIY tasks, the preparation work takes time and care, but it pays dividends in the end.

Marking up and clearing the site

Mark the shape of the area to be surfaced using pegs and brightly coloured string or builder's spray marker. Check the corners are set at right angles using a builder's square. If you're putting the surfacing beside your house, you'll need to locate your damp-proof course (*see* right).

Next, you'll need to remove the existing surface material from the site. If you're stripping off turf, undercut it using a spade, then stack it away in a corner of the garden to use for topsoil later (*see* page 36). You could hire a turf-cutter for larger areas of grass, to make the job easier.

If you're removing an old patio or path, which can be very hard work, you'll probably need the help of a hammer drill available from a tool-hire shop, or get a contractor to do it for you. Get rid of the waste straight away in a skip. The existing foundations might be usable, but if not, put them in the skip too.

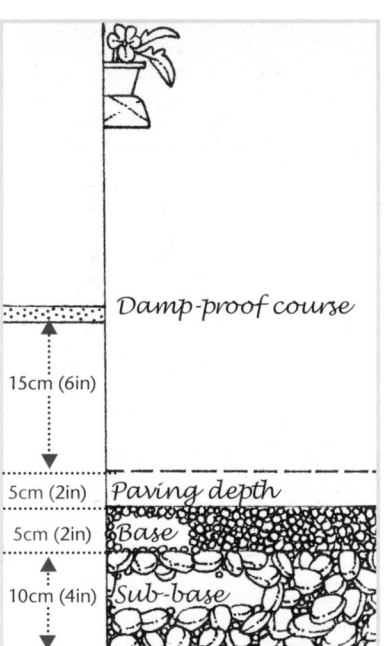

Damp-proof course

15cm (6in)

5cm (2in) *Paving depth*

5cm (2in) *Base*

10cm (4in) *Sub-base*

For a patio beside your house it's vital to dig deep enough to have space for the foundation layers without risking compromising the damp-proof course. Allow about 15cm (6in) for the various foundation layers and then the same distance again from the top of the paving to the damp-proof course.

To make a gravel path you need to excavate the site, compact the soil and add a sub-base of hardcore, scalpings or hoggin before topping with gravel. For a heavily used paved area, you should add an extra base layer such as sand or concrete.

Excavating the site

Once you've cleared the site it's time to excavate it. If you're digging an area near the house, the depth to dig to depends on the height of your damp-proof course. Add together the depth of the foundation layers (usually about 15cm/6in; *see* page 74) and the depth of the surfacing material (for instance the paving slabs) and make sure the damp-proof course will still be 15cm (6in) above this (*see* left). For larger areas, you may choose to hire a mini-digger for the task.

Setting the levels

To set the level of the foundations, you'll need wooden pegs (about 30cm/12in long), a spirit level and a long, straight plank of wood.

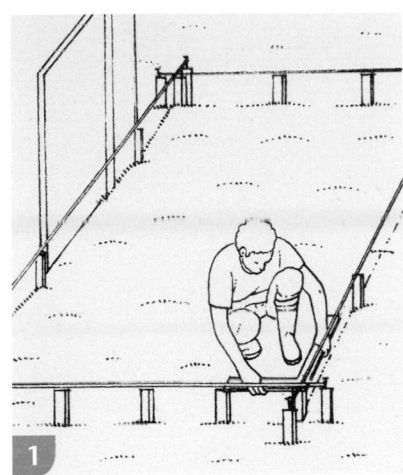

Mark out the perimeter of the area for the new patio or path with pegs driven into the ground and string lines. Hammer nails into the corner pegs and secure the string to these. Use a builder's square to check that the corners are at right angles.

Dig to a depth of around 15cm (6in), depending on the height of your damp-proof course and thickness of paving (*see* opposite). If the soil is loose, tamp down the area using a plate compactor (*see* page 71). Remove the pegs and string.

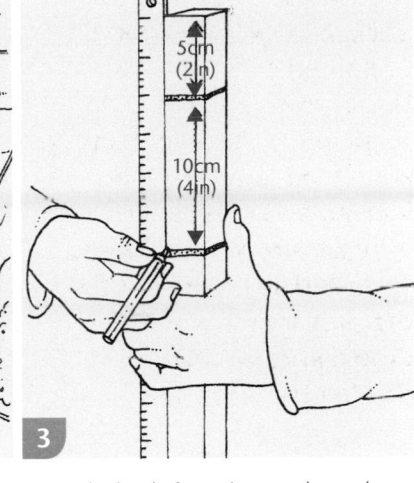

To set the level of a patio or path, mark up a set of 30cm (12in) pegs on all four sides to show the depth of the combined foundation materials, usually 15cm (6in). You'll need enough pegs to cover the base of the site at 2m (6ft) intervals.

For a patio, drive a row of marked pegs 2m (6ft) apart into the ground along the side nearest the house. Insert them up to the lower line marked in the previous step. Check that the area between the pegs is level by using a long, straight plank of wood and a spirit level. To make a path, set the pegs along either side of the route and check the levels in the same way. You do not need to set a fall for a path, so proceed to step 6.

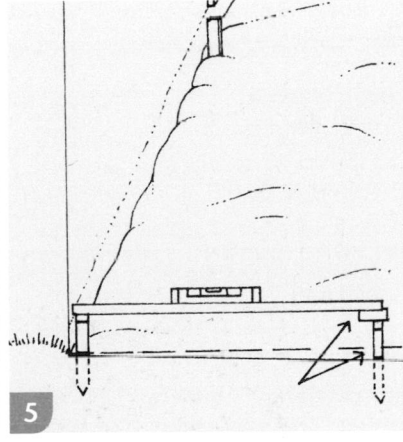

For a patio, you'll need to set a fall (*see* page 74). Insert a second row of pegs 2m (6ft) from the first, away from the house. Place a small wood offcut, about 25mm (1in) thick, on top of a peg in row two and use a spirit level and the plank to check the levels. Lower the peg in row two until the spirit level reads level. Repeat this along the line of pegs – from row one to row two and row two to row three and so on.

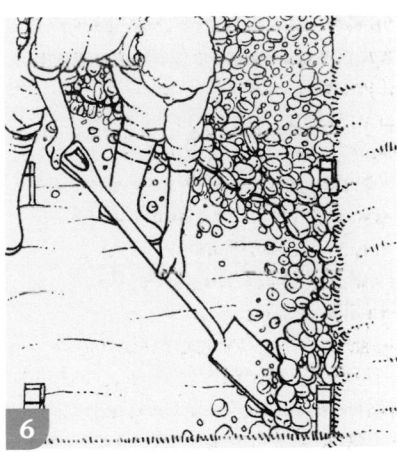

Rake the site until you can see the lower marked lines on all the pegs. This ensures the base of the site is parallel with the final patio surface. Add the sub-base such as a layer of hardcore up to the top line marked on the pegs. Compact this with a plate compactor. Now add the base layer. If you're using sand, compact it until the foundation is level with the tops of the pegs. Once the base is laid you're ready to add your paving slabs or other surface.

Levelling pegs can be purchased from DIY stores under a variety of names, but otherwise you can make them from 25mm (1in) square wooden battens.

For a patio, you'll need to make a grid using the pegs. For paths, use the pegs to mark out the route, setting them along either side. In both cases, use them to level the ground using a straight plank and a spirit level. The tops of the pegs will indicate the final level of the surfacing material.

Making a fall

With a patio, you'll have to allow for a slight slope or 'fall' so that rainwater is shed off the patio and away from the house. If there's a suitable drain, you could slope the patio towards this, otherwise slope it so the water is shed off into the garden. You need a slope of about 2.5cm (1in) for every 2m (6ft).

You don't usually need to set a fall for a path, but if you want a gently sloping path, use the technique for creating a fall (see page 73, step 5).

Adding the foundation materials

Once you've dug to the correct depth and set the levels, work over the area with a plate compactor (see page 71) to settle the soil, so there's no chance of it settling unevenly. For a really firm, long-lasting base that supports heavy loads, you need to put down two foundation layers, the sub-base and the base, before laying the final surface. This ensures that the surface will be firm enough to support a path or patio without the paving stones or bricks shifting.

Sub-base layer

The sub-base may be made from hardcore (a waste building material, such as old bricks, broken up into smallish pieces). Other materials include scalpings (any loose material made up of stones of different sizes, up to about 4cm/1¾in) and hoggin (a mixture of clay, sand and gravel that compacts well and provides a stable, low-cost base).

First, spread the sub-base material evenly over the excavated area and then compact it well, again using the plate compactor. This layer should be about 10cm (4in) thick when you've finished working on it. On a relatively unstable soil, such as sand or clay, you'd be advised to make it 15cm (6in) thick. Conversely, for areas that won't receive much use, or where the soil base is firm and already very well compacted, 8cm (3in) thick will suffice.

Base layer

After laying the sub-base, you need to spread the second layer (known as the base layer) on top. For paved or brick paths and patios, this layer should be about 5cm (2in) thick when it has been compacted. This second layer is not necessary when using gravel or other loose surfaces.

For paving slabs the base is often made from sharp sand, which makes a smooth, even surface. It may also be made from concrete (see Recipe 1, right), which makes a rough, level base for smaller surfacing materials, such as bricks. Once the base layer is laid you're ready to add your final layer. (For poured concrete see pages 85–6, for paving and brickwork see pages 75–81.)

Recipes

Below are some basic recipes you'll need to use as binding agents and/or as foundations when constructing areas of hard surfacing. It's easiest to mix ingredients by volume. Gravel and sand together are known as 'aggregate'.

RECIPE 1 – WET CONCRETE
Wet concrete is ideal for setting bricks firmly onto a hardcore foundation. Added plasticizer ensures it is easily workable before it sets.
- 3½ parts coarse gravel
- 2½ parts sharp sand
- 1 part cement
- A little plasticizer

RECIPE 2 – BEDDING MORTAR
A fairly soft mortar that is used to form a strong bond with concrete paving slabs and other surfaces.
- 5 parts sharp sand
- 1 part cement

RECIPE 3 – GROUTING MIX
This mixture is used dry, which means it can be swept into tiny nooks and crannies. It sets to a tough grout, usually by absorbing atmospheric moisture, though it can be watered in.
- 3 parts soft sand
- 1 part cement

RECIPE 4 – POURING CONCRETE
Pouring concrete is an all-purpose mixture that has a wide range of uses, such as for paths, hard-standings and making foundations. It soon sets to a hard, durable surface.
- 2½ parts coarse gravel
- 1½ parts sharp sand
- 1 part cement

RECIPE 5 – BRICKLAYING MORTAR
Bricklaying mortar is used to join bricks together. It has a small amount of plasticizer added, which makes it softer and more maleable.
- 3 parts soft sand
- 1 part masonry cement (this has plasticizer added to make it more workable; if you use ordinary cement, add plasticizer).

Paving and brickwork

Paving can be laid on patios, terraces, in courtyards, along paths and around other features in the garden, such as a pond, greenhouse or shed. In a small garden, you may well pave over the entire area, perhaps leaving space for trees, shrubs or a flower bed. This is often a more attractive solution than trying to have a lawn the size of a pocket handkerchief, particularly if the space is heavily used.

Choosing paving

Surfaces can be paved with a wide variety of materials, such as stone, brick, concrete, terracotta and ceramic. Natural stone is particularly effective in its place of origin, but York stone, marble, slate and granite are at home wherever they are used. Bricks are valued for their colour and versatility (*see* pages 78–81). They

This straight, paved path along the front of a house has been punctuated with rows of bricks, which slow the progress of your eye to the gate.

make wonderful edging and are ideal for breaking up larger areas of paving slabs. Ceramic and terracotta tiles are often chosen to recreate some of the atmosphere of a particular place, such as the Mediterranean, Morocco, the Caribbean or India. Among paving materials, concrete is the least expensive, as well as being the most utilitarian, but it is also the most versatile.

A contemporary dark-slate patio is beautifully counterbalanced by lush, traditional planting.

Decorative detailing

Instead of having a path or patio consisting wholly of paving slabs, it's very effective to introduce decorative details using smaller-size materials. For example, to create interest and provide additional colour and texture you could leave out a few paving slabs from your patio and fill the empty areas with cobbles (*see* page 89), glass pebbles, marbles, pieces of flint, broken tiling or pottery – the sky's the limit. Simply fill the space with bedding mortar (*see* Recipe 2, page 74) and press your choice of material down until it's level with the rest of the surface. For a softer effect, use plants between the stones (*see* pages 110–1).

These paving stones were probably originally intended to make a circular patio, but they become altogether more interesting when combined with dimpled bottle bases in a swirling pathway.

Laying paving

Before you buy paving, carefully measure the area to be surfaced. If you can be slightly flexible about the size of your patio, or width of your path, it's worth adapting it to keep cutting to a minimum, as it's a time-consuming and not particularly enjoyable job (*see* steps 2–4, opposite). It's often a good idea to allow a small margin of gravel beside the house, about 10–15cm (4–6in) wide, to ensure adequate drainage and keep the wall dry. You could

The weather-worn terracotta paving of a meticulously laid patio produces an interesting play of light in this dappled corner.

also use this space to plant climbers up the house wall.

Paving stones and bricks must be laid on a firm, level base, so thorough preparation of the area is essential (*see* pages 72–4). Don't forget to include a fall to ensure that surface water drains away from the house and into the garden.

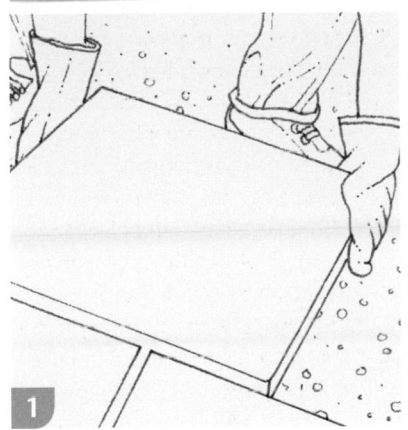

1 Prepare the site (*see* pages 72–4). Cover the sub-base with a 50mm (2in) layer of sharp sand. Set the paving about 18mm (¾in) below the level of surrounding turf. To check the fit, lay out the slabs 'dry' in your chosen pattern, leaving a gap of 10mm (½in) between slabs.

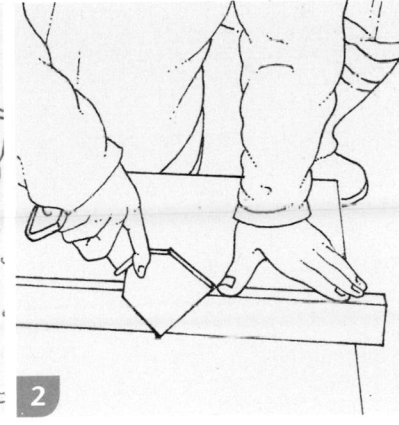

2 Ideally, you will have planned for the area to be laid with whole slabs only, but you may need to cut paving slabs to fill gaps. Place the slab to be cut on a firm, flat surface. Use a piece of wood as a straight edge and score a groove to mark the cutting line using a bolster chisel.

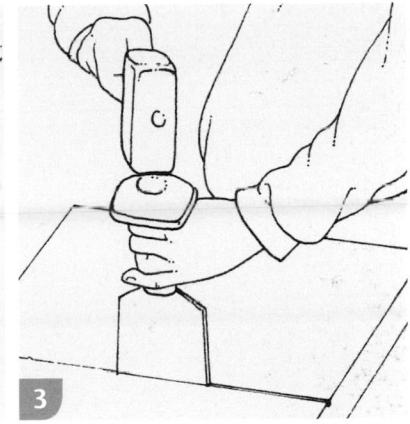

3 Holding the bolster chisel in one hand and a club hammer in the other, work along the scored line, tapping the chisel lightly with the hammer. Make a groove a few millimetres deep, then continue the groove down both edges and across the underside of the slab.

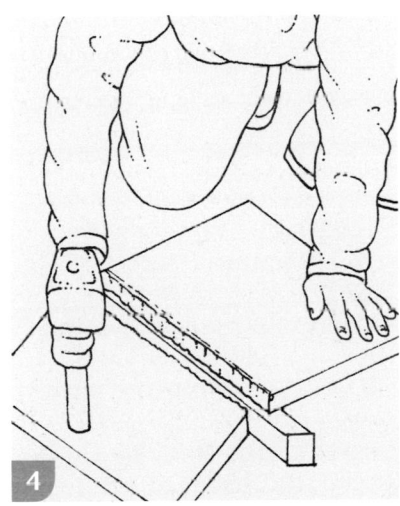

4 Place the slab on a piece of timber over a firm, flat surface. Align the groove with the edge of the wood and tap the slab with the handle of the hammer until the paving slab breaks in two. Tidy up the rough edges with the bolster chisel if necessary. For a completely clean cut, you could hire a stone splitter. Wear goggles to protect your eyes from flying concrete splinters.

5 Mix the mortar (*see* Recipe 2, page 74). A small barrow-load at a time should be about the right quantity to mix so you can use it up before it sets. Make the mix quite sloppy. Lay the slabs a few at a time, setting them to one side while you spread the mortar. The mortar layer should be about 50–60mm (2–2½in) deep, worked with a trowel to make a ridged surface, which will help with levelling the slabs.

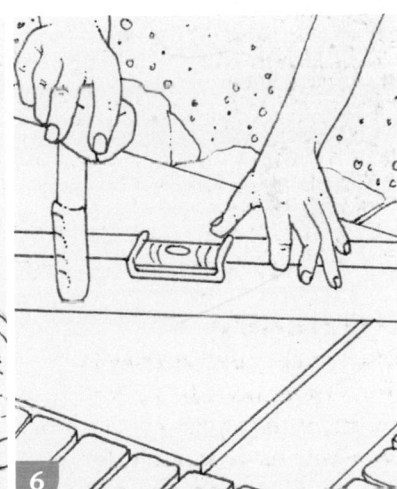

6 Rest the first slab on the mortar and gently tap it level with the hammer handle. Repeat with the other slabs. Keep off the paving for at least 24 hours to allow the mortar to set. Fill the joints with grouting mix (*see* Recipe 3, page 74), pushing it in between the slabs with a gloved hand and leaving no gaps or cracks. Finish the joints with a raking or pointing tool to give a neat finish and sweep away the surplus mix.

A patio and path of seemingly ancient bricks help to underline this garden's formality without disturbing its lush, tranquil atmosphere.

Brickwork

Bricks are a useful and attractive surface and are available in a range of colours; they can be combined with paving stones on a patio or to edge a path, or used on their own. Their small size means that they're easier to use than paving slabs for making small or curved shapes, which is why they're particularly useful for paths.

You can't use just any brick to make paths and patios. Those that are fine for walls may not be able to take the constant wetting and drying

This combination of red bricks and grey pebbles that form this surface makes a bold statement. The brick edging prevents a cluttered effect.

or frost and cold weather that they will be exposed to on the ground. Choose engineering bricks for this type of situation. Make sure that your brick surfaces won't spend many hours in the shade every day, as they're prone to growing algae, which makes them very slippery.

Think carefully about the pattern of the bricks and the effect that you want to create before you start. They offer so much scope for interesting and varied patterns, including parquet, herringbone or basketweave designs (*see* page 80). To lay bricks as a flat surface, follow the instructions for laying paving slabs (*see* page 77).

Raised beds and walls

You may like to incorporate raised beds (*see also* page 116) or planters in your patio, and to create a sense of unity you could use the same bricks for the horizontal and vertical surfaces. If you make the beds chair-seat height, they'll make excellent perching places for you to enjoy your morning coffee or something stronger on a summer's evening.

Building vertical constructions with bricks is a lot more difficult than laying them on a flat surface. Bricklaying for retaining or load-bearing walls is best left to a professional, but you may want to have a go at making a low wall or small raised bed to enhance the patio – it's certainly more satisfying and less expensive to do it yourself.

Foundations and drainage

Brick structures such as walls and raised beds must be built on very firm foundations. If the wall or raised bed is going to be on an existing

A brick pathway runs between raised beds enclosed by low brick walls, increasing the sense of privacy around this wooden hideaway.

paved patio, you can simply lay the bricks on top of the paving without adding a foundation layer. Otherwise, you need to provide a footing (*see* pages 83–4). The centre of the beds must be unpaved to allow the soil in the bed to drain freely, so if you're building raised beds on an existing patio, you'll need to remove some slabs from the centre.

Steps, low walls and simple stone benches are combined to create this sunken water garden. The generous overhanging planting provides shelter and seclusion.

It's easy to make the surface of a patio or path interesting and attractive by laying paving slabs or bricks in a pattern. Unlike brick walls, which must be bonded in particular ways for stability, brick patios or paths can be laid in any pattern you like. Traditional patterns range from simply staggered joints for functional paving to intricate, interlocking designs, which are often used for brick surfaces and those made from natural stone.

A parquet design has a classic feel.

Brickwork

Bricks and block pavers (also called engineering bricks) are relatively small, so laying them end on end or side by side produces a fussy effect that isn't usually what's wanted over a large surface area. To avoid this, they're normally arranged in groups of two, four or more, to make strong visual patterns that are easier on the eye. So it has come about that bricks and small pavers are laid in recognized sequences with descriptive names such as basketweave and herringbone.

It's worth bearing in mind that some patterns require less cutting than others. With herringbone, for example, the entire perimeter of the patio will be finished with cut bricks, while with parquet you might get away with cutting only a very few. It's a good idea to make a dry run over a small area to check how it will all work out.

Stone and concrete paving

Natural stone paving usually comes in rectangles and squares in a variety of sizes. This enables the quarries to make economic use of the stone they have available. Fitting the paving together is rather like doing a jigsaw puzzle and there will usually be some cutting to be done, but it's one of the loveliest surfaces and the end result is always worth it.

Concrete paving slabs are available in myriad shapes and sizes that can be laid in any number of patterns. There

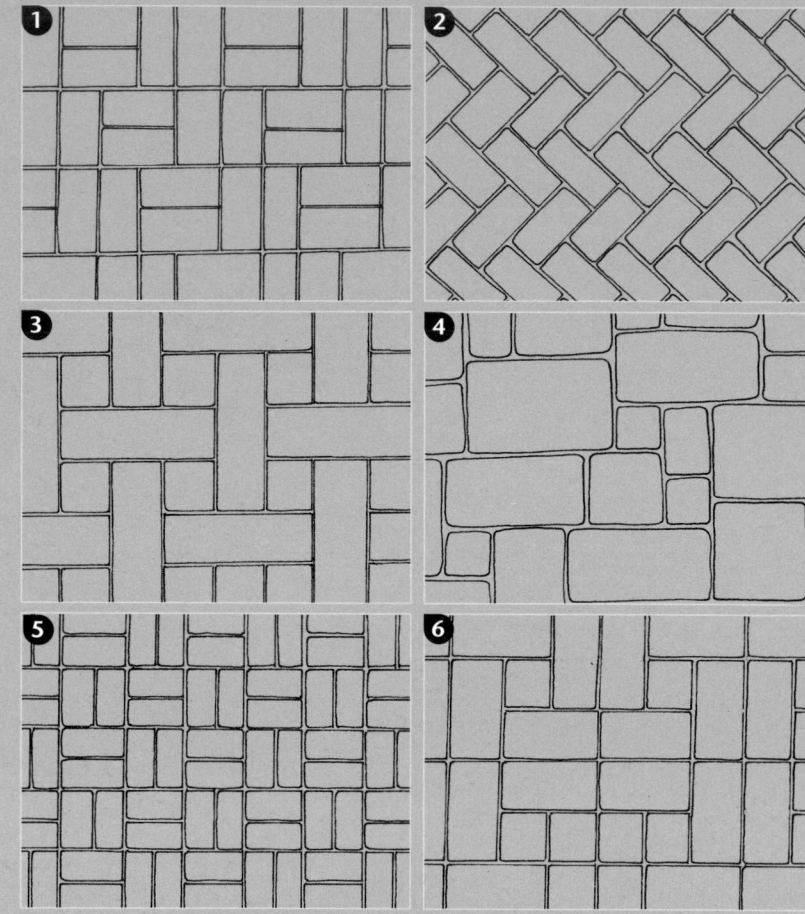

are slabs that mimic brick surfaces and those that look like terracotta tiles, setts, cobbles, natural stone or even wood. You can buy kits of paving slabs that allow you to make a hexagon or a circle without having to do any cutting, and some have patterns set into them for interesting finishes.

Bricks form geometric patterns and can be laid on their edge or face downwards showing the wide surface. Stone patterns are random and pieced together.
① Staggered basketweave (brick)
② Angled herringbone (brick)
③ Latticework pavers
④ Irregular natural stone
⑤ Regular parquet (brick)
⑥ Interlocking pavers

![photo of a garden patio with paved area, outdoor dining table and chairs, surrounded by shrubs and topiary]

Laying the bricks With bricklaying you work towards the centre, so with a wall you start at the ends and work inwards; with a raised bed you begin by making the corners, putting two bricks at right angles to each other and building in both directions with each course.

First, mix up some bricklaying mortar (*see* Recipe 5, page 74) and spread a 10mm (½in) layer along the concrete foundations to the required width. Lay the first brick, using a spirit level to check for correct alignment, then 'butter' the end of the second brick with mortar and butt it up to the first. Tap each brick gently with the trowel handle to level it. Once the first course is laid, start to build upwards, again from the corners or the ends, checking

Bricks on their edges have been used to add interest to the paving and to edge patio beds. A low brick wall echoes the theme and separates the patio from the rest of the garden.

that each course is level and that the sides are vertical and the bricks aligned. Start the second course with a brick cut in half, to stagger the joints. As you fill in the courses, continue to check that everything is level using a spirit level. Keep the mortar joints to a constant width to ensure the bricks will fit without further cutting. Finally, smooth the joints and clean off any mortar residue from the sides of the wall.

When the raised bed or wall is as high as you want it, cap it with cut bricks or coping slabs to prevent water from damaging the top.

Bricks combine with paving to create interesting patterns and textures and provide a useful edging for the lawn.

If your garden has a slope or if there's a drop between your patio and the lawn, the perfect solution is to install a flight of steps, or even just a single step. As well as serving a practical purpose, steps can be an attractive design feature, tempting you out into the garden or drawing attention to a particular area of interest.

Paving slabs, natural stone, concrete and bricks can be used alone or in combination to make steps, and the work doesn't have to be as difficult as you might think. In fact, if you've read this far, you already know something about all the techniques you need – you just have to put them into practice. The steps shown and described opposite are made from brick risers and paving-slab treads, which is one of the most straightforward ways to make steps. In an informal situation, you could use railway sleepers to make the

Just because steps are functional it doesn't mean they can't be decorative too.
① Sleepers and gravel make a slightly rustic but very serviceable flight of steps.
② Concrete pavers are easily softened with sympathetic planting.
③ These tiled steps are rather daring!
④ This dazzling set of spiral steps, made from blue concrete, is a real eye-catcher.

HOW TO make steps

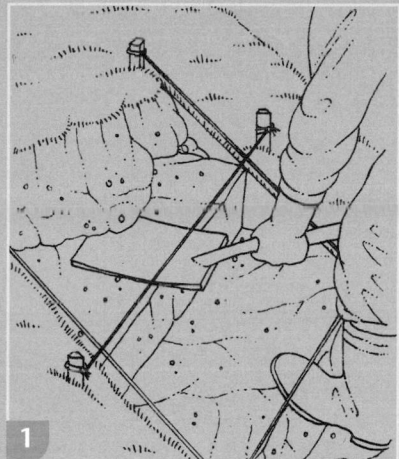

1

Use string and wooden pegs to mark out the position of the steps and the front of each tread. Make sure that the height of the risers and depth of the treads correspond to the materials you plan to use, such as bricks and paving stones. Using a spade, dig out the shapes of the steps in the soil. Compact the soil.

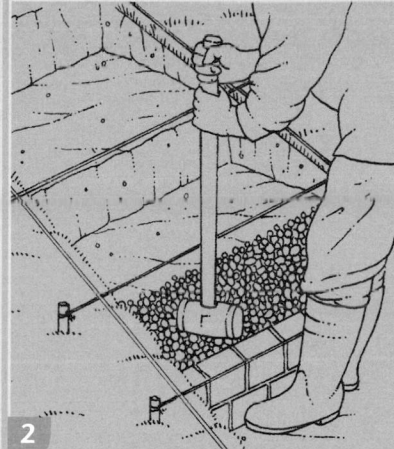

2

Starting at the bottom of the flight, make a concrete footing (*see* below). Allow this to set before laying the brick courses to make the first riser using standard bricklaying methods (*see* page 81). Check its alignment using a spirit level. When the risers have set, fill the area behind with well-compacted hardcore until it is level.

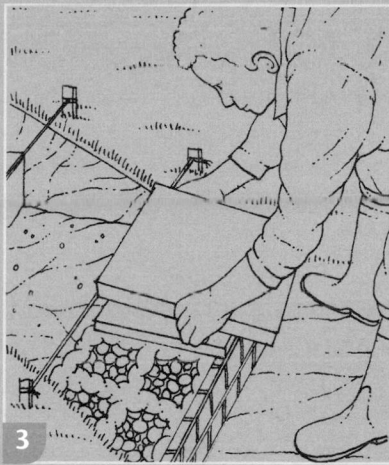

3

Place mortar on the riser and hardcore and position the tread. Construct the next riser at the back of the tread. Continue in this way until the final tread is flush with the surface at the top, then brush grouting mix (*see* Recipe 3, page 74) between the paving stones. Refill gaps around the edges of the steps with soil (you can turf or plant it later).

risers, although you should bear in mind that they can get slippery so it's worth using another material for the treads, such as gravel (*see* opposite).

Measuring and footings

To calculate the number of steps you'll need, first measure the slope and record the measurements (*see* page 23). For short, sharp slopes, stretch a piece of string from a wooden peg on the top of the slope to a cane at the bottom, ensure the string is level and

Don't forget

Ideally, risers should be not more than 10–15cm (4–6in) high; treads should be not less than 30cm (12in) from front to back. There should be a very slight fall (about 1cm/½in) to the nosing (front of the tread) to ensure rapid water run-off, which avoids dangerous slipperiness.

the cane vertical and then measure the height at which the string touches the cane. Divide this figure by the height of a riser. Of course, on longer slopes you might choose to have clusters of steps and 'landings' between them to make the descent more interesting.

Railway sleepers can be laid directly on the soil or onto a layer of hardcore for drainage, but bricks or blocks require a foundation, or footing (*see* page 84), to ensure the steps will be level and don't collapse or sink. Position the footing under the first riser. Make a trench 30cm (12in) wide and 10–15cm (4–6in) deep and fill it with a layer of compacted hardcore 5–10cm (2–4in) deep. Cover this with a layer of wet concrete mix (*see* Recipe 1, page 74) about 5cm (2in) deep. Ensure the footing is level using a spirit level.

Bolivian black slate has been used to make these classy steps, which lead seamlessly onto a patio made from the same material.

Terracing and retaining walls

If you want a patio and your garden is steeply sloped, you may have no alternative but to move earth in order to produce a single flat area (or terrace) at the top or bottom. You might also consider terracing the whole garden. A series of flat areas connected by steps and separated by retaining walls is certainly easier to cultivate than a single steep slope.

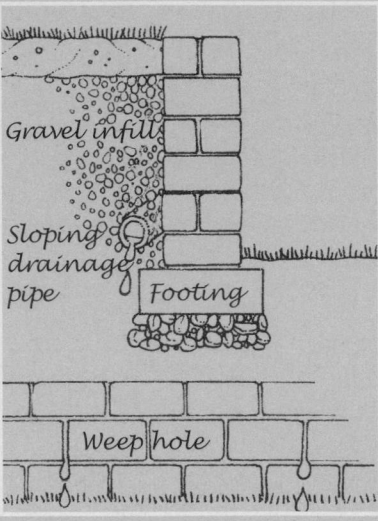

Retaining walls must be built on a firm, concrete footing and should be very sturdy – a double row of bricks at least. A gravel infill and sloping drainpipe or weep holes in the mortar ensure each terrace drains freely.

Practical but beautiful, the terracing – made from wood and brick with abundant planting – is the making of this garden.

The amount of work involved in terracing should not be underestimated. Below are some basic instructions on how to create terracing, but unless you're very confident about construction, it's usually best to call in a contractor, as it helps to have specialist equipment, additional labour and expert advice. There are also safety considerations – not the least being risking the integrity of your home through subsidence.

Creating terraces and retaining walls

First, you should do some very careful diagrams and calculations. You need to measure the slope (*see* page 23) and plan the surface area of the terraces and the height of any retaining walls. Also, work out how much soil you're going to be moving.

Before you start to level the areas, you'll need to remove the topsoil and store it somewhere, otherwise you'll end up burying your topsoil and having subsoil, which isn't a good growing medium, on the surface. Before you lay any bricks you'll need to build a concrete footing under ground (*see* illustration, above, and page 83).

The walls that support terracing are often made of bricks or even concrete blocks faced with stone or rendered. With solid walling materials, you need to allow for drainage (*see* illustration, above). If you're planning a modern garden, it's well worth considering gabions (wire nets filled with stones) to do the job of retaining, as they're ready

made, very sturdy (they're used on motorways after all) and readily allow water through. Railway sleepers are also suitable and age beautifully within a couple of years.

Plants for retaining walls

Some of the most attractive retaining walls are made with natural stone, and if mortar is not used in the gaps between them, they provide the perfect situation for a variety of plants, including two infamous campanulas – *C. portenschlagiana* (dark-blue bells) and *C. poscharskyana* (light-blue stars). These two little plants come in for a lot of flack, but they're superb in this situation and happily fill a large area within a relatively short space of time. Other good wall plants include the smaller variegated ivies, some lewisias and other rock-garden plants. Ideally, limit your choice of plants to two or three types to avoid a busy effect.

Concrete surfaces

Concrete is a popular choice for utilitarian areas in the garden and elsewhere, including driveways, largely because it's inexpensive, hardwearing and easy to lay. Although it's not considered the most beautiful of surfaces, it can be coloured or textured to make it more attractive; brushing the surface while it's drying will reveal the aggregate, which can make for interesting finishes. It's also a very versatile material that can be formed into almost any shape you want.

Mixing and laying concrete

Concrete consists of cement and fine particles of stone, including pebbles and sand, known as aggregate. The dry ingredients are mixed with water to create a chemical reaction that binds the aggregate into a hard, dense material.

You can mix smaller amounts of concrete yourself by hand in large buckets, or you can hire a small cement mixer. Combine the dry ingredients (see Recipe 4, page 74) and then gradually add water until the consistency is firm but not stiff.

Don't forget

Temperature change causes concrete to expand and contract. To prevent cracking, it's worth adding a permanent expansion joint in areas greater than 4m (13ft) wide or long, or 2m (6ft) long in the case of a path. Use thin strips of treated wood and insert them into the shuttering before pouring the concrete.

Concrete has a simple beauty. Here, the wood used to produce these concrete forms has added texture and a ribbon of thyme softens the area.

If you're dealing with larger amounts (for instance if you need a lot for a large patio or driveway) it's easier to buy in ready-mixed concrete. Always discuss your requirements with the supplier, and bear in mind once the load is delivered you'll have to finish the job within a few hours.

Before you start you'll need to have marked up, cleared and excavated the site thoroughly (see pages 72–4) and made the shuttering (see page 86). You'll probably need another pair of hands during the laying process.

HOW TO lay concrete

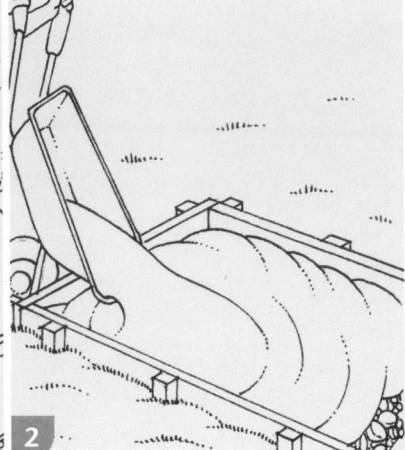

1 Excavate the ground to 15cm (6in) (*see* pages 72–4) and lay a hardcore sub-base to a depth of 10cm (4in). This hardcore could consist of hoggin (a gravel and sand mix) or crushed brick or stone. Rake it level, break up any large lumps, then tamp it down using a sledgehammer, heavy piece of wood or a plate compactor.

2 Mix the concrete as near to the site as possible and transport it to the shuttering (*see* below). Starting from one end of the site, pour the concrete over the sub-base and spread it up to the corners and edges of the shuttering. Fill the shuttering and rake the concrete roughly level until it is just proud of the edges of the boards.

3 Compact the concrete by chopping along the surface in an up-and-down motion using a plank. Fill any low spots or gaps. Go back over the surface, sliding the plank from side to side, removing excess concrete and smoothing the surface. Cover the surface with a weighted plastic sheet. After about a week remove the plastic and shuttering.

Shuttering

When using pouring concrete, you'll need to install 'shuttering' – a retaining formwork that keeps the wet concrete within bounds. To make shuttering, set long, straight wooden boards – ideally 25mm (1in) thick – on their edge marking out the area to be filled, and hold them in place by nailing them to 50mm (2in) wooden stakes (*see* above). Remove the shuttering after the concrete sets hard.

Instead of laying solid concrete – in a driveway for instance – you could set strips of concrete into grass: the concrete takes the weight of the car and the grass absorbs rainwater and reduces the chance of flooding.

Hybrid surfaces

It's not very environmentally friendly to concrete over your front garden for car parking and it also increases the risk of flooding in periods of heavy rainfall (*see* page 13). Instead, you might consider installing a hybrid system, which is a greener alternative.

A hybrid surface is made up of pre-formed concrete blocks with a waffle or egg-box design. The weight of a car or pedestrian traffic is borne on the upper parts of the block and soil is brushed into the lower parts, which act as planting pockets for grass. This construction allows rain to soak down into the soil, so that the grass can grow well and suffers minimal damage from the weight of a car, for example. The grass is cut with a hover-type mower that simply passes over the blocks. It's inadvisable to use a traditional cylinder mower because it might catch its blades on the blocks.

Some systems allow gravel, decorative aggregates or bark to be used instead of grass – all of these allow water to sink into the soil beneath.

Gravel and other loose materials

There's a wide variety of surfacing materials that could be called 'loose' and they're excellent for both small and large areas, being easy to lay and producing a textured and coloured finish. They're more flexible than hard surfaces and offer a more informal finish. They can also be used in conjunction with paving, stonework, concrete or bricks for added interest.

Choosing loose materials

The range of loose surfaces available includes gravel, slate, scree, cobbles, pebbles and bark chippings, to name but a few. As with other hard surfaces, your choice will depend on the look you want to achieve, the type and size of area to be covered and your budget. Loose materials are available in almost any quantity, from small bags to lorry loads of several tons – discuss your requirements with your local hard landscaping merchant or stone quarry, or try a garden centre.

Gravel and slate

Gravel is a very versatile surface covering and it will fit neatly into any gap, no matter how small or awkward. It really comes into its own if you need to fill in small spaces such as those between the patio and the house. In a small area

In this pretty cottage garden the gravel takes the place of a lawn, filling the open spaces and softening the surrounding planting. Its textured surface absorbs light, adding to the sense of intimacy and enclosure.

Slate chippings and gravel can be combined to produce interesting effects in small spaces, as in this little corner of my old garden at Barleywood.

like this, gravel is perfect as it allows water to drain away from the house and avoids you having to cut tiny pieces of paving to fit right up to the walls. Gravel is also useful for larger areas, such as driveways, and it makes a great alternative to a lawn in a small garden (*see* above).

Don't forget

Avoid using gravel and other loose surfaces up to the edge of the lawn. Some stones will inevitably get caught up in the mower, which can be dangerous if they flick up as the blade catches them, or they can even break the blade itself. Always use an edging to keep the stones and grass separate (*see* page 47).

Plants can seed themselves in gravel, spreading and producing a lovely, natural effect.

In addition, gravel is a useful material for deterring unwanted visitors, because it makes a crunching noise as you move across it. If you surround your house with a thick layer of gravel it would be a brave burglar who tried to creep across it. By the same token, you might not be so popular with the neighbours if you regularly drive over it first thing in the morning.

You can buy gravel in a range of colours, grades and textures, including grey, red, white and yellow. It may be large or small and rounded (pea shingle) or in the form of flatter chippings, so you're bound to be able to find something to suit your design and surroundings. Slate gravel or chippings comes in blue, grey or green, so it's ideal for

The complexity of this gravel garden, enclosed by concrete walls and a rill, has been balanced by restrained planting, including rosemary and ornamental grasses.

creating a cool, relaxing theme. Chippings are flatter than most gravels, so they bed down more easily and are more comfortable to walk on, making them a suitable surface for paths and small patio areas. You could lay an area of smaller chippings beside larger ones for a naturalistic effect.

Scree

Scree forms naturally below rock faces: the weather erodes the rock and the small pieces fall away to accumulate as a slope at the base. In the garden, the name implies rough, smaller stones of uneven size that are larger in size than gravel. Like gravel, scree comes in a range of shades so you'll be able to choose a colour to match your garden

A swirl of blue chippings emerging from an ammonite fossil makes a pleasing and surprising focal point in this Oriental-style gravel garden.

Gravel combines with wooden blocks to make a checkerboard pattern. The colours are harmonious and the different textures provide interest.

scheme. Because of its larger size, it's useful for blending the hard landscaping of the drive or patio into the garden. With a scree area, roughly grading the stones from large to small adds to the naturalistic impression. You could fix the largest stones into bedding mortar (*see* Recipe 2, page 74), to keep them firmly in place.

Ornamental stones and cobbles

The smooth, rounded surface of ornamental pebbles renders them attractive to adults and children alike. They're a popular decorative material, although they're relatively expensive – pricier than rough stone for example – but you don't need many to make an impact in a small area. They're available in a range of sizes and colours and are particularly effective around pools and water features, where the splash of the water ensures their colours are revealed as brightly as possible.

Any stone larger than an egg is usually classed as a cobble and, like ornamental pebbles, cobbles vary in shape and colour. Since they're expensive to use on their own, they're usually used as accents, combined with other materials, such as complementary stones of a smaller size. For example, if you're planning to create a path that runs gently through the garden and is more of a feature than a functional throughway, you could fill the centre with inexpensive paving slabs or setts and edge it with cobbles. Alternatively, you could use a gravel filling to give the path an even less formal appearance.

Where a formal path would be inappropriate, such as through this woodland border, bark provides the ideal surface and is easily replenished.

Rockery stone consists of larger pieces of rough stone in a range of attractive colours that you can use, like the cobbles, to make a feature (*see* page 90) or as edging to an area. For instance, you could use it as a rustic edging to a sloping path or flower beds.

Bark chippings

Bark produces a soft surface and is very popular for informal paths in the garden (*see* above) as well as a mulch. It's inexpensive, easy to transport and very simple to lay. Bark makes a good surface for children's play areas, but it must be checked regularly because it can be popular with local cats, who use

Larger loose materials, such as cobbles, can be set into mortar or sand to create a more stable surface and produce a mosaic effect.

it as a litter tray. It's not ideal near the house, as you'll tend to walk it inside, and it's a favourite with blackbirds, which can scatter it in the search for food. Bark surfaces will need weeding from time to time and will need topping up after three or four years.

Laying loose materials

To lay a loose surface, dig out and prepare the area in much the same way that you would prepare a surface for paving or brick (*see* pages 72–4). However, you don't need to worry so much about levelling, nor providing a fall, as the water will simply drain through.

Define the perimeter of the area to be surfaced using edging. For a gravel drive, for example, kerbstones would work well and keep the gravel within bounds, whereas for a bark path you might prefer an informal border of rockery stones or even rough logs or round fencing posts.

By combining large and small elements it is possible to achieve radically different results: an informal, almost soft effect with pebbles and pea shingle (above left) and a strongly structured, linear surface of slate and granite chippings (above right).

Whenever you disturb soil, you bring weed seeds to the surface, which gives them enough light to germinate, so it's advisable to use a weedproof membrane under any loose landscaping materials. Choose the thicker variety and make sure you tamp the soil down well,

removing larger stones before laying it. Use a plate compactor (*see* page 71), if necessary. Weeds will eventually find their way into loose surfaces but if the membrane is tough enough they won't be able to put their roots down very far and will be easy to remove.

Aftercare

Loose materials have a habit of travelling and settling and therefore need topping up from time to time. This is more likely to happen with bark, which also rots down. The plus side is you can easily and quickly refresh your gravelled or scree area without a major overhaul being necessary. You can even rework its shape and borders without having to take everything up and start again.

Boulders and pebbles play a large part in the success of this modern take on a rock garden, with drifts of plants and gravel adding to the picture.

Decking

Wood is an extremely versatile natural material that not only looks good but also feels great under your hands and feet. It's incredibly useful in gardens, where it's found in the form of decking. There's so much potential with decking – it can be used to create a surface at almost any height as well as any shape or size, and it can fit into the most awkward corner or straddle the most uneven piece of ground.

Like so many other good ideas, decking has gone through a phase of overexposure and overuse that has dented its reputation somewhat. Over-popularity resulted in decking being used in inappropriate situations, which in turn led to it being blamed, often unjustly, for all sorts of ills. The resulting bad publicity meant it fell from favour almost as fast as it had risen. The fact is that, as with any other type of hard surfacing, there are places where decking is ideal and areas where it should never be considered.

To deck or not to deck …

If you think about the nature of decking, and the qualities of wood, you can tell where this surface will be most useful. Wood is relatively light compared to paving, so decking is a good choice on a balcony or roof, where you want an attractive surface but where weight is an issue (see pages 16 and 94–5). The fact that decking can be constructed on a frame and lifted

into place means that it can be laid on top of an existing hard surface without breaking up and removing the old one. Also, it's built on posts of any length, so it's ideal for creating a platform raised above ground or placed over an uneven or sloping area of ground without undertaking major structural alterations.

By the same token, you should be able to make a pretty safe bet about where it really will not do well. Even when pressure-treated, wood will decay if the conditions are less than ideal. For example, if the area is subject to a lot of wet from dripping trees or if it spends most of the day in the shade, the wood will grow algae, become slippery and start to

This decking area works as a true extension of the house, with wide-opening French windows allowing a seamless connection between the inside and the outside.

rot. A good airflow around, above and below the decking will certainly help, but in this type of situation you'll need to give it a blast with a pressure washer from time to time to keep algae to a minimum. Alternatively, cover the walked-on surfaces with a layer of chicken wire.

The other major criticism laid at the feet of decking is that it attracts vermin. But this shouldn't be the case if it's well constructed on a suitable frame. Vermin won't make themselves at home if their every

Lush bamboos planted in galvanized-metal raised beds surround this roof terrace, creating a private space that is large enough to accommodate a table and chairs.

twining sensuously around the balustrades; on a steamy day, you could imagine you're in the middle of the jungle. Alternatively, you can create the impression of being beside water by constructing a length of decking that resembles a pier or jetty, using weathered boards and stout upright posts. The handrails could be made of rope and the whole effect complemented by shells, sand and/or pebbles and plants that recall the seaside.

Because it is relatively light, and easy to install and remove, decking is one of the most suitable materials for a roof terrace. It can be made to sit slightly off the main roof surface so as not to interfere with rainwater drainage systems, and is easily cut to fit around other roof features, such as chimneys. With sensible provisos, such as having your plans checked by a structural engineer and if necessary strengthening the area, there is no reason why most flat roofs cannot be converted into an additional living space, much appreciated in a city, but full of possibilities in the countryside, too.

Optical illusions

You can manipulate your impression of the space by using narrow decking boards to make the area seem wider or broad boards to make it seem smaller. Laying the boards diagonally or in a straight pattern running away from the main viewing position (such as your patio doors) will make the area seem more spacious. Conversely, laying the boards from side to side across the area can make a long, narrow plot seem wider and shorter. This is

A vibrant Mediterranean-style deck is enhanced by a pretty vine-covered pergola that provides dappled shade.

move can be scrutinized from above, or if they can't gain access in the first place. If you're concerned about the possibility of unwanted tenants, position the deck high enough off the ground that you can get rid of them, if necessary.

Design possibilities

Your deck can be any shape, size or design you want, so give your imagination free rein. For instance, you may like to create a tropical feel in the garden – you could raise the deck up on stilt-high posts and grow lush, large-leaved trees and shrubs beneath and beside the deck and plant up containers with exotic-looking plants, including climbers particularly useful in a long, thin garden, as it makes the space seem more in proportion, giving you the sense that the far end of the garden is nearer than it is and reducing the 'runway' effect.

Alternatively, rather than having one large, single area of decking, you can install several different blocks at different heights (*see* pages 17 and 69) or even separated by short walkways. This is particularly successful as a replacement for lawn in a small garden that is all on one level, and it diverts attention away from the limitations of the size.

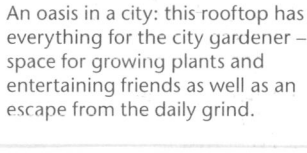

An oasis in a city: this rooftop has everything for the city gardener – space for growing plants and entertaining friends as well as an escape from the daily grind.

Create a living area

A wooden deck creates the feeling of an outdoor room and an extension of the house probably more than any other type of hard surfacing. For this reason, you can use furniture, lighting and other furnishings that may look out of place in other parts of the garden.

Seating and storage areas are easily incorporated into the overall structure of a deck, adding to its usefulness and saving space elsewhere. You can create a box-like storage space beneath the seats for garden tools, cushions or play equipment, accessed by lifting the seat. Or, with a raised deck, put the storage facilities below and get at them via a hatch or small door. Such storage areas need to be waterproofed with heavy-duty plastic sheeting.

With its log-fire grill, generous built-in seating and space for a large rectangular table, this outdoor kitchen-diner is the hub of the home in the summer.

Pergolas and balustrades

You might decide to build a pergola-type construction over part of the decking (*see* page 92). This will provide you with shelter from the sun and a frame for climbing and other plants. Pergolas are readily available as kits and are easy to install or you can design your own. Once the pergola is in place, the choice of climbers to grow up it is vast – consider a rose, clematis or even a grapevine (*see* page 92).

Another design consideration is a balustrade or simple handrail. Of course, railings are vital on a raised deck, where they should be set at 1.2m (4ft) above the deck level, and vertical slats or balusters should also be added to prevent children from falling through. However, balustrades are worth considering even if you're creating a low-level deck. As well as giving you the opportunity to add decorative detailing, they also provide vertical interest, which can be important if the decking area is large and flat and on one level, and they provide a boundary between the garden and deck.

Making a plan

If you're planning anything more than a straightforward square or rectangle of decking, it's worth making a scale drawing of your intentions (*see* page 23). This way, you can see where problem areas are going to be, how to avoid undue cutting of timber and any other details that will need special attention. Go to the timber merchant's or DIY store and find out the dimensions of the timber that you intend to use (*see* right and opposite) and spend some time drawing everything out.

Remember to mark the joists – positioned about 45cm (18in) apart, around and within the frame; they create the main structure and strength of the deck. Also mark the support posts – these will be at each corner and at 1.5m (5ft) intervals around the deck frame. With large decks, you'll need them within the frame too.

With decks that stand more than 60cm (24in) above the ground, it's advisable to seek the advice of a structural engineer, who will be able to work out load-bearing calculations. You don't want to build a lovely deck only to have it collapse, damaging your house wall as it goes. The same goes for balcony and rooftop decking – it's absolutely vital to ensure your existing building is strong enough to take any additional loads. Also, check with your local council offices to make sure you don't need planning permission to build your creation.

Buying the timber

It's very easy to buy the various components, ready cut, grooved and shaped, to make decking. They're often sold as a pick-and-mix kit. If you plan to put decking in an area that's under trees or shaded for much of the day, it's a good idea to select these ready-made decking boards, as the grooves speed up drainage and improve foot grip when they are wet. However, if you want something more unusual, you can choose your own timber.

Steep steps lead to this decked terrace, which is enclosed by a simple wooden balustrade that complements the trellis fencing both beside and below it.

Don't forget

Always check the source of your timber before buying, so you can be certain you aren't contributing to deforestation or unethical or environmentally unfriendly harvesting practices.

Wood types

For outdoor use, wood for decking should be at least 2.5–5cm (1–2in) thick to prevent it from twisting or warping as it gets wet and dries out. Other than this, you can have any size of timber you want, from railway sleepers downwards.

Decking comes in two varieties: hardwood and softwood. Hardwood is the more expensive option, but it's longer lasting and tougher. Softwood is much cheaper but will need more attention, without which it passes its best in about five years.

Hardwoods include teak and oak. The trees these woods come from grow slowly and so as a result the wood is much more dense, which is why it's so tough. But it's the slow growth that makes it pricey. Green (unseasoned) oak is particularly long

lasting, but can be very expensive to buy, even when recycled, and may twist and warp with age. Pine, on the other hand, is a fast-growing softwood and so is much more plentiful, making it cheaper.

Nowadays, no one can claim to be unaware of the problems caused by inappropriate harvesting of hardwoods from vulnerable rainforests. If you choose to build your deck with hardwood, please make sure that the timber is from forests that are carefully managed with a full programme of replacement planting – such woods usually carry a tag. A reputable timber merchant or DIY centre should be able to tell you where their wood comes from and if they can't, then shop elsewhere. Softwood should also come from a properly managed source.

The faded grey of the decking used to create this outdoor space softens its appearance and it seems to float on its own reflection in a perfect marriage of texture and form.

Treating wood

Make sure that whatever wood you choose has been treated with preservative; pressure- or vacuum-treating ensures that the preservative has penetrated deep into the wood. Buy your wood from a reputable timber merchant to ensure that you're getting the best – poorly treated timber won't last.

Don't forget

Even if the timber has been treated prior to purchase, it will need painting with wood preservative or paint every year.

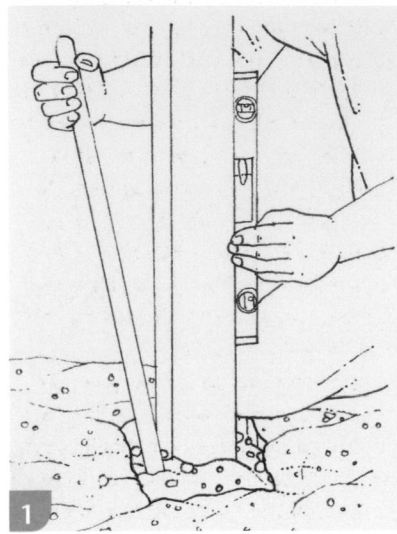 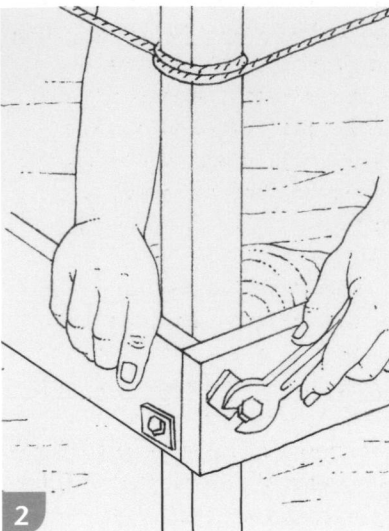 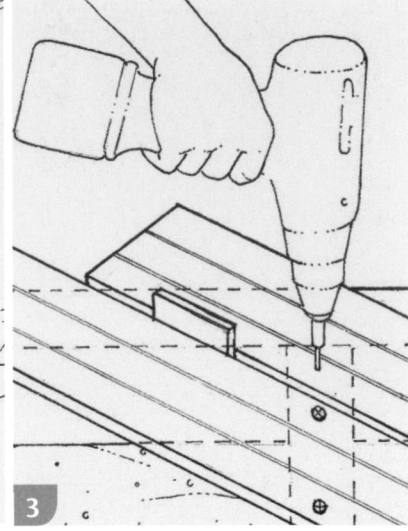

1 For each support post needed for a ground-level deck, dig a hole 30cm (12in) square (with higher decks, the depth needs to be 45cm/18in). In the bottom of the hole, put broken bricks, hardcore or a concrete building block. Set the post in the middle and pour in a stiff concrete mix around it (see box and illustration, opposite). Check it is vertical using a spirit level. Leave the concrete to set (about two days).

2 To make the frame, use galvanized coach bolts to fasten the outermost joists to the support posts at the required height. Keep checking with a builder's square and spirit level to make sure the frame is level and perfectly square. Nail, screw or use joist hangers to fit intermediate joists between the main outer ones at a distance of 45cm (18in) apart. Stagger noggins between these, at intervals of 1.2–2m (4–6ft).

3 Attach the decking boards to the joists, leaving a gap of about 5mm (¼in) between each board – use slivers of wood as spacers to make the job quicker and use countersunk screws for a neat finish. The planks should overhang the edge of the frame by at least 5cm (2in). When you have screwed them all in place, draw a line along the edge at the overhang and trim off any surplus with a saw.

Laying decking

In many ways, decking is easier to construct than a paving-slab patio. The key to getting it right is to set the levelling posts into the ground at the correct depth and to take the time to make sure the frame is properly constructed. It's also very important to make sure that the nails, screws and coach bolts you intend to use are all the correct length and suitably strong. Once you have the frame in place, laying the boards is straightforward.

With a raised deck or a deck on a slope, you'll be able to see beneath the decking, unless you close in the sides with boarding. In an open situation like this, you may choose to cover the visible area with a suitable mulch of gravel, bark or other loose surface (see pages 87–90) or even add some plants later, in which case you'll need to make sure they have some good soil to grow in between the support posts.

Preparing the site

Preparation of the site and the amount of work involved depends on the height of the deck and the surface it's going on to. If you're installing a low deck that's going on top of an old patio or on a balcony or roof, you just need to give the area a sweep and make sure it's level and stable. However, if it's going on to bare ground, there's considerably more work to do.

First, you'll need to find and mark all utility supplies and mark out the area using wooden pegs and string (see page 25). Kill perennial weeds and cover the soil surface with a weed-suppressing membrane. The area must drain well; if it doesn't,

Don't forget
It's quicker and easier to adjust the level of the deck and ensure its frame is completely sturdy before you add the decking boards.

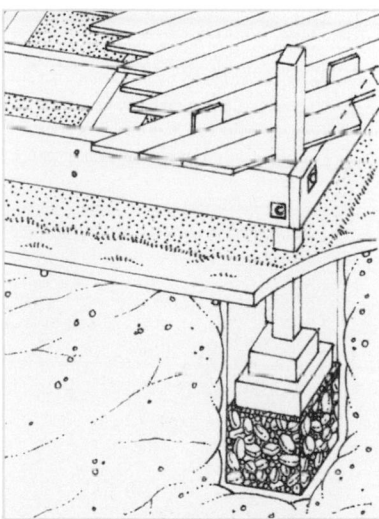

Decking is constructed on posts, which must be securely concreted into the ground, but it is otherwise simply made of wood, bolts and screws/nails.

Large, blue-green decking steps lead to a gravelled area full of drought- and salt-tolerant plants in this delightful, sunny seaside garden.

consider putting in additional drainage (*see* pages 33–4). With a ground-level deck, for a long-lasting job in a site that has less than perfect drainage, it's well worth digging out the whole area to a depth of about 10cm (4in) and backfilling it with compressed hardcore (*see* step 1, page 86).

Installing the decking

First, mark up the positions of the support posts and then set them in place with concrete (*see* box, left). They must be vertical and secure (*see* step 1, opposite, and left). Don't worry if you're building on uneven ground, as the posts can be trimmed to the same height when the deck frame is made. Simply make sure that the post that is in the lowest position is at least as tall as the level of the deck surface.

Next, you need to make the frame (*see* step 2, opposite). If you're particularly worried about water lying on the deck surface, you can incorporate a slight fall when you fit the deck frame (*see* step 5, page 73). Choose the direction of the fall and add a small slope to the appropriate outer framing joists. At this stage, if you're installing a ground-level deck, it's a good idea to make the area beneath the deck unwelcoming to small animals by filling the spaces between the joists with gravel, to make it difficult for them to nest comfortably, even if they manage to make their way in.

Once you've done this, you can lay the decking boards (*see* step 3, opposite). Work systematically from one side of the deck, laying out the boards in the direction you want them and attaching them to the joists using nails or, for a neater finish, countersunk screws.

Finally, when the deck is in place, you can paint the wood. If there are plants near by, make sure you use a plant-friendly, water-based paint that won't cause them or garden wildlife any harm.

Plants for lawns and hard surfaces

A lawn offers a wonderful opportunity for planting, whether it's a specimen tree or shrub, a swathe of spring bulbs or a variety of wildflowers. The larger the lawn, the greater the scope, but even small lawns will complement the plants you choose. Patios, decks and other hard surfaces – even roofs – cry out for the softening effect of plants. Raised beds and containers are excellent ways of introducing greenery, but you can also furnish the edges with tall or overhanging plants, such as shrubs, climbers and small trees, to create a feeling of seclusion and intimacy.

Trees and shrubs for lawns

There's something truly majestic about trees, so try to include at least one in your garden if you can. They add visual interest in the form of height, colour and structure, provide shade and shelter and attract birds to the garden. A tree or even a specimen shrub planted in a lawn can be a really striking focal point, drawing the eye from a large expanse of green. Along with all their other plus points, once they're established trees and shrubs don't need much looking after.

A white-barked birch off centre in a level lawn provides a focal point in the corner of this garden. It casts only gentle shade, enabling the grass to grow up to its trunk.

Placing trees in a lawn

Probably one of the hardest things about choosing trees for your lawn is to limit yourself to just one or two specimens among the wealth of varieties that are available, but you really do need to do this to be successful. You can opt for a single, striking specimen to be viewed from all sides. Or, if you want to include a few, bear in mind that they tend to look better grouped together as a mini copse rather than being scattered randomly around the lawn.

While it's a very popular thing to do, planting a tree in a lawn is not always easy to get right. Whatever you do, don't plonk it right in the middle of the lawn; it will never look good that way. Unless you're aiming for a very formal garden, trees are much better placed off centre.

From a vantage point in the house or on the patio, look down the lawn and into the distance beyond – can you see anything you'd rather not? Or is there a neighbour's window looking directly into your garden? Try to position your tree so that it reduces the impact of eyesores or frames something you would like to draw attention to. If you're lucky enough to have a view of the countryside, two or three trees together might help to link your garden with these surroundings, while in a city or town a tree at the end of the lawn could give the impression of space and greenery beyond, even where there is none.

Deciduous feature trees

In a small lawn you need a tree that provides interest for most if not all of the year. It is not enough to have one outstanding ornamental feature, such as lovely flowers, autumn colour or berries – a tree needs to

Cornus kousa var. chinensis in full bloom. The clear circle of soil around its trunk avoids patchy grass growth.

have a number of decorative features that span two or more seasons as well as an attractive habit. Cornus kousa (see above) is a great multi-seasonal tree, with white, flower-like bracts in early

Prunus × subhirtella 'Pendula Plena Rosea' is a weeping ornamental cherry with rose-pink flowers in spring and yellow autumn foliage.

summer, followed by red fruits and crimson leaves in autumn. It also has attractive flaking bark and an upright to spreading habit. Many crab apples (*Malus*) have pretty flowers as well as ornamental fruits, and are good for smallish areas. *Sorbus cashmiriana* has many-leafleted leaves and white flowers, followed by pink or white berries on a neatly spreading tree.

Trees with interesting bark, such as the paper-bark maple (*Acer griseum*), snake-bark maple (*A. pensylvanicum*), silver birch (particularly *Betula utilis* var. *jacquemontii*) and the Tibetan cherry (*Prunus serrula*) also make a great focal point in a lawn (*see* box, opposite). None of these trees grows too fast, too dense (which would kill the grass) or too huge (which would produce too much shade), so they're ideal.

For autumn colour, there are few trees that can beat *Acer palmatum* (*see* below), with its lobed leaves that turn bright crimson in autumn. There are many varieties available in a range of habits. Many cherries (*Prunus*), for instance *P.* 'Okame' and *P. sargentii*, also have good autumn foliage as well as attractive flowers.

Trees with a particularly neat habit include *Pyrus salicifolia* (*see* opposite), which has silvery, willow-like foliage on a rounded tree and creamy-white flowers in spring, and its weeping form *P. salicifolia* var. *orientalis* 'Pendula'; there is also the mop-head acacia *Robinia pseudoacacia* 'Umbraculifera' with attractive leaflets. Make sure you get this variety if you want a small tree, as the other forms can be very large.

Evergreen feature trees

Evergreens can also be effective in a lawn, particularly those with variegated or golden foliage that contrasts with the grass. *Taxus baccata* 'Fastigiata' is an upright,

Other trees for lawns

Catalpa bignonioides 'Aurea'
Cercis siliquastrum
Fagus sylvatica 'Dawyck Gold'
Genista aetnensis
Koelreuteria paniculata
Magnolia obovata

Don't forget

For more natural-looking areas of lawn – perhaps in areas of longer grass, where you intend to naturalize bulbs or grow wildflowers (*see* pages 105–9) – choose species that blend in with the surrounding landscape rather than selecting non-native varieties or highly bred cultivars, which may look out of place.

Japanese maples are renowned for their autumn foliage, but many also have a lovely habit with fine, sinewy branches. This is *Acer palmatum* in its autumn finery.

In this quirky garden, the silvery leaves of *Pyrus salicifolia* provide an interesting contrast to the evergreen topiary yews while its neat shape complements them.

Ornamental bark

In the dead of winter when the leaves have fallen, tree trunks stand out in the garden; some have startlingly decorative bark.

① *Acer griseum* – flaking, red-brown bark and a spreading habit.

② *Prunus serrula* – shiny, mahogany-brown bark that peels in strips, white flowers and a rounded, lollypop-like habit.

③ *Acer pensylvanicum* – green bark streaked with white and an upright habit.

④ *Betula utilis* var. *jacquemontii* – chalk-white peeling bark on a slow-growing, upright tree.

columnar yew with bright-yellow foliage. It's slow growing and makes an excellent specimen, as does *Picea pungens* 'Koster', a lovely spruce with silver-blue leaves on stout stems and a conical shape. *Pinus sylvestris* 'Watereri' is a short, slow-growing Scots pine with stiff, blue-grey needles and a spreading habit. For an evergreen with a light touch you can't go far wrong with *Pittosporum tenuifolium* 'Silver Queen' – a compact, round-headed tree with grey-green, white-margined leaves.

One of the best evergreen trees, because it has so many seasons of interest, is *Arbutus* × *andrachnoides* – it has attractive, red-brown peeling bark, glossy-green evergreen leaves, white flowers followed by fruits and an upright then spreading habit.

Areas under trees

If you're planting a tree in a lawn, bear in mind that you'll have to cut the grass around the tree somehow, and that it will lose its leaves in autumn if it's deciduous.

You can get around the mowing problem by creating a circular bed around the base of the tree; make it large enough to cut the grass without damaging the trunk. Initially, you can plant in this area, but as the tree gets bigger, it will become a very dry spot because the leaves act as an umbrella and the tree itself takes up most of the available moisture. If you want to plant beneath as the tree matures, you'll need to choose your plants carefully (*see* page 102–3). Weeping (or pendulous) trees, which have

A gnarled specimen of *Prunus* 'Shirotae' spreads over a bed of evergreen elephant's ears: an unusual but effective combination.

Shade-tolerant plants for growing under trees

Bulbs

Anemone

Cyclamen

Eranthis (winter aconite)

Erythronium (dog's tooth violet)

Galanthus (snowdrop)

Hyacinthoides (bluebell)

Sclla

Trillium (wood lily)

Perennials

Anemone

Astilbe

Bergenia (elephant's ear)

Digitalis (foxglove)

Epimedium

Euphorbia amygdaloides subsp. *robbiae* (wood spurge)

Hosta

Climbers

Actinidia kolomikta

Clematis alpina or *C. macropetala* cultivars

Eccremocarpus scaber (Chilean glory flower)

Humulus lupulus 'Aureus' (golden hop)

Lathyrus latifolius (perennial pea)

Lonicera (honeysuckle)

Rosa (rose)

Tropaeolum speciosum (flame nasturtium)

branches that bend downwards towards the ground, such as a weeping cherry or birch, look very graceful when planted in isolation and are justly popular specimen trees. However, their form creates much more shade than trees with a more upright habit, which is not good news for the grass underneath.

Planting under trees

Some trees are ideal for under-planting because they create only light canopies, which allow plenty of sun through to the ground beneath. The birches, such as the Himalayan

birch (*Betula utilis* var. *jacquemontii*), are particularly good as they have sparse and small leaves. However, most trees produce dense canopies, limiting the choice of plants that can grow beneath. One of the best options in this case is to plant spring bulbs, since these grow, flower and die back before the trees' leaves

Creating a striking feature in a late winter garden, this small group of silver birches in my lawn at Barleywood is simply underplanted with snowdrops.

Don't forget

The area under trees will be fairly dry and will lack nutrients, so you'll need to feed regularly (*see* pages 48–50).

create too much shade. Alternatively, select shade-loving ground cover or low, spreading plants (*see* box, left). In the case of evergreen trees, make do with their own decorative effects, or use one as part of an island bed and plant outside its shade.

When choosing plants to go under a specimen tree in a lawn, avoid shrubs and larger plants. These tend to conceal the trunk and shape of the tree. However, trees in lawns make excellent hosts for climbers (*see* box, opposite) – the

A wonderful, ancient juniper makes a magnificent specimen in this lawn. When young it would have grown very low to the ground, hiding any suffering grass.

Birch trees are deservedly popular in lawns – here the peeling trunks of *Betula nigra* 'Heritage' are corralled by curved benches.

trunk and branches provide support for the climber and the climber decorates the trunk with flowers. You'll need to match the vigour and strength of the climber to the tree – for small specimen trees avoid very vigorous climbers.

Shrubs in lawns

If you don't have space for a tree, choose a shrub or even two or three. Some shrubs have an upright habit and can be pruned to look like a multi-stemmed tree. If you have the space, planting a shrub as a specimen in the lawn is a great way to enjoy a particular favourite, because you can see the whole plant. It, in turn, can grow unhindered by neighbours that compete for light, water and food so it will develop to its full potential.

In a lawn, shrubs have the same advantages and disadvantages as trees, but many also lack a clear trunk, so their foliage reaches to the

ground, with the obvious side-effect that the grass will suffer. Two things could happen: the grass around the perimeter of the shrub grows long and lanky due to the lawn mower not reaching it, or the grass gets shaded out and dies. With the former, get out a pair of shears and neaten the area; with the latter, create a bed around the shrub and either make it bigger each year as the shrub grows, or prune the shrub to keep it within bounds – the choice depends on the shrub and whether it can take such regular pruning without beginning to look deformed.

Feature shrubs for lawns

Amelanchier lamarckii
Ceanothus thyrsiflorus 'Skylark'
Cotinus coggygria 'Royal Purple'
Daphne odora 'Aureomarginata'
Philadelphus 'Belle Etoile'
Pieris formosa var. *forrestii* 'Wakehurst'
Viburnum plicatum f. *tomentosum* 'Mariesii'

Planting and feeding

The best time to plant a shrub or a tree (*see* right) is autumn to early spring, but not when the soil is hard. If it's any later you must be prepared to do plenty of watering.

Ornamental plants, such as trees and shrubs, have different fertilizer requirements to grass, so it's important to cater for both. Grass needs a fertilizer that is high in nitrogen (N) for healthy leaf growth, but too much nitrogen will push trees and shrubs towards leaf growth at the expense of flowers and fruit. They need a balanced fertilizer (equal quantities of NPK, *see* page 48) or if they're to flower or fruit one that is higher in potassium (K). Fork fertilizer lightly into the soil around the plant and give it a thorough watering to make sure it gets into the root zone. Keep the area below the tree weed free.

If you have a fruit tree in a lawn, either leave a large area around the trunk so you can feed it well, or don't feed the grass around the tree at all. Otherwise you may find the tree produces fewer and fewer flowers and fruit.

Leaves and leaf mould

Leaves generate a great deal of heat as they decay, so they must be removed from the lawn as they fall in autumn; if left, they will literally cook the grass. Collect them up and put them in pierced plastic bags (old compost bags or bin bags). This allows them to rot down into leaf mould, which is a good soil improver for use around the rest of the garden. They need to rot for at least six months before you use them, so stand the bags in an out-of-the-way place. Make sure the leaves are damp when the bag is full and simply fold the top over to trap the moisture inside.

HOW TO plant a tree or large shrub in a lawn

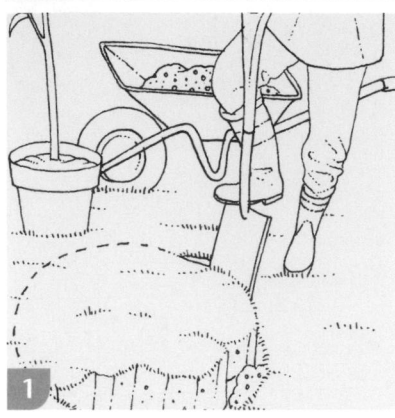

1 Make a planting hole about 1.2m (4ft) across – it should be at least four times the diameter of the pot the tree or shrub came in, or its rootball if you bought a bare-rooted tree. Remove the turf first and stack it for rotting down (*see* page 36), then dig out the soil, putting it into a wheelbarrow or onto a piece of plastic sheeting to avoid messing up your lawn. Make the hole about one and a half times the depth of the pot.

2 If the plant's compost is very dry, stand the pot in a bucket of water until it's very moist. Add garden compost or any other organic matter (such as a couple of bucketfuls of well-rotted manure) to the base of the hole and fork over the soil to mix it in. Also fork organic matter into the soil that you removed from the hole. The idea is to have a good moisture-retentive mix in which to plant your tree or shrub, not simply garden soil.

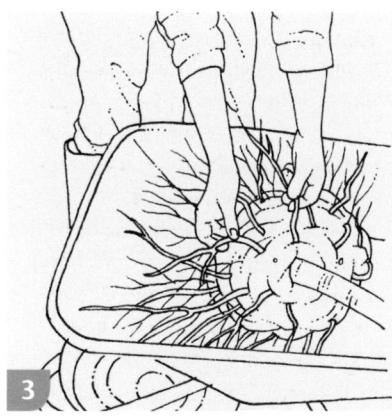

3 If the plant's roots have filled the pot, tease them out a bit all around to encourage them to break out from the pot shape and into the soil around them. Place the tree or shrub centrally in the hole, adding some of the compost–soil mixture if necessary to bring the top of the tree's rootball just about level with the soil surface. Backfill around the tree with the soil and compost mixture, firming it in well as you go.

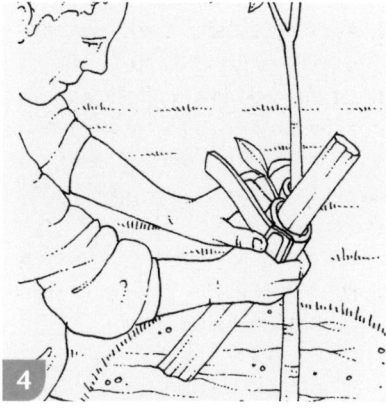

4 Most trees need a stake for the first couple of years, while they are getting properly rooted in. Making sure you miss the rootball, hammer in a stake of about 1–1.2m (3–4ft) long at an angle of 45 degrees to the ground, near enough to the tree to secure it with a proper tree tie. The top of the stake should point in the direction of the prevailing wind. Water the tree or shrub in very well – a couple or three watering cans is not excessive.

Flowers for lawns

Although the traditional lawn should consist only of grass species, if you're a relaxed sort of gardener and if you aren't bothered about having a high-quality sward, you may like to try developing a wildflower lawn or naturalizing bulbs in the turf. If you have a large garden, you could include a more traditional lawn as well as a wilder area where you can leave the grass longer and let flowers spread. A natural-style lawn can look stunning and is also great for wildlife.

Sometimes it really is possible to achieve more by doing less: in this case, more flowers by doing less mowing.

Naturalizing bulbs in lawns

It can be fun and decorative to grow bulbous plants such as fritillaries (*Fritillaria meleagris, see* right) and crocuses in your lawn. Many of those we grow in our garden borders today have been bred from species that occur naturally at a woodland edge or in a meadow; in the right conditions, they will thrive and multiply in garden grass, giving a wonderful display every year with very little input from you.

For the sake of simplicity in gardening books, bulbs, corms and tubers are often lumped together as bulbous plants. They're quite similar in that they all produce growth from a storage organ (the bulb, corm or tuber) and mostly the growth dies down to this after flowering, although in some plants (such as many alliums) the leaves die before flowering. Many flower early in the

year, including daffodils (*Narcissus*) and snowdrops (*Galanthus*), others late in the year, including naked ladies (*Colchicum*) and winter aconites (*Eranthis hyemalis*), but it is the dying down of the whole plant that makes bulbous plants so good for growing in lawns – once the foliage has disappeared the grass can be tended as normal.

If you have a tiny lawn or use it regularly all year round, don't try to naturalize bulbs. The foliage of spring-flowering varieties starts appearing above the ground in winter and the area cannot then be mowed or stepped on until six weeks after the flowers have died down. The ideal is to choose a quiet

Snake's head fritillaries flower on long stalks in early spring. Growing bulbs in lawns requires an easy-going attitude to mowing, but it pays dividends.

Don't forget

Before buying, find out whether your choice of bulbs will grow where you want to put them. Don't assume that the obvious place for them is under a tree or on a grassy slope – a sun-lover won't like it under a tree and a moisture-lover will hate a well-drained bank.

A pondside at the height of its beauty, with hosts of daffodils surrounding a weeping cherry. After the blooms are over, mowing will return all to a neat state.

area that you pass often or can see from the house, so you will enjoy the flowers when they appear but won't find they get in the way.

Choosing bulbs for lawns

Specialist bulb suppliers can recommend varieties that are suitable for naturalizing. As a rule, keep it simple to make the planting look natural. Stick to one or two varieties rather than many different types, and avoid having lots of different colours side by side. If it wouldn't happen in nature, it shouldn't happen in your garden. That's not to say you can't have a succession of flowers in the same place if you want to. For instance, crocuses (*see* right) or snowdrops

Crocuses produce a mass of blooms in spring, opening wide to reveal their yellow stigmas and style.

can be followed by daffodils (*see* above) in the same area. Some species are more suitable for naturalizing than highly bred cultivars – for instance, species daffodils of the 'I wandered lonely as a cloud…' variety generally have small flowers atop shortish stems and suit planting in grass. However, over the years, plant breeders have selected some of their offspring to make new varieties with bigger, brighter flowers on thicker, longer stems, which suit borders and are good for cutting, but don't look as 'natural' in grass as their forebears.

Don't forget

Scattering handfuls of bulbs and planting them where they fall gives an informal look, making the flowers appear as though they had popped up naturally. Ideally, they should be one bulb's width apart.

How to plant bulbs in lawns

Ideally, plant in drifts or groups of uneven numbers, so the flowers look as if they've spread naturally over the years – never in straight rows. If you buy your bulbs in bulk, there may be a variety of sizes, some of which will be ready to flower and others not, and this will contribute to the natural effect. When you plant, allow each bulb enough room to grow and multiply. If you don't do this, the bulbs will soon become crowded, and crowded bulbs are less likely to flower, so you'll have to dig them up and divide them within a few years.

There are various different ways to plant the bulbs. You'll need to plant larger bulbs individually, using a trowel or bulb planter, which cuts out neat plugs of turf and soil to a depth of about 10–15cm (4–6in). If you have lots of smaller bulbs, it's quicker and easier to lift a whole section of turf and plant a group of bulbs beneath (*see* below).

The best way to plant smaller bulbs, such as crocuses and fritillaries, is to slice back a piece of turf and pop several bulbs underneath. Return the turf, firm it down well and water the area so that the grass doesn't suffer.

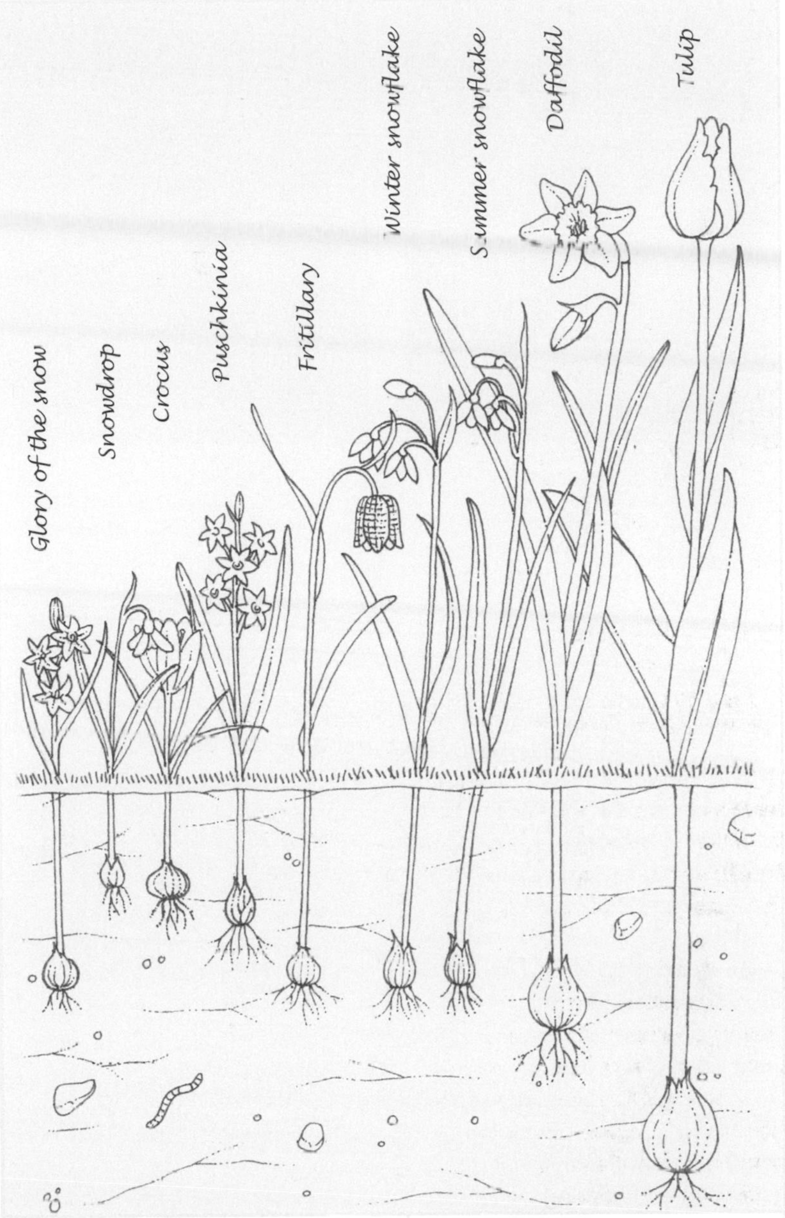

A general guide is to plant bulbs at a depth equal to three times their height. Planting is traditionally done in autumn, but snowdrops are best planted after they have flowered but while they still have their foliage. Tulips can be planted until midwinter.

Glory of the snow — Snowdrop — Crocus — Puschkinia — Fritillary — Winter snowflake — Summer snowflake — Daffodil — Tulip

Cowslips are delicate creatures and won't withstand close mowing, so plant them at the lawn margins.

Clover thrives in grass and its fragrant flowers, produced in spring or summer, are popular with bees.

When to feed bulbs

The fertilizer that a lawn needs to grow well can encourage bulbs to grow leaves rather than to flower. Grass needs a high-nitrogen (N) fertilizer during its main growing season to promote strong, vigorous leaf growth, but where you have bulbs, it's important to wait until their leaves have completely died down before you apply this. Before the bulb leaves die down, feed them a fertilizer that is high in potassium (K) to help them set flower buds for the following year. This will not hurt the grass – in fact, it slows the grass growth down slightly, which is no bad thing when you can't cut it anyway.

Creating a wildflower lawn

A wildflower lawn involves encouraging a range of wildflowers to grow in your sward. If you already have a well-established grass lawn, to make a start on a wildflower lawn simply stop mowing your grass quite as closely. Cutting it to 5cm (2in) long, rather than 2.5cm (1in), enables a range of low-growing plants, such as bird's foot trefoil, self-heal, round-leaved speedwell and clovers, to make a comeback. Many people regard these as weeds, but weeds are only ever plants growing in the wrong place, so if you actively want them, you won't classify them as such.

If your lawn has been well tended for a long time, these small wildflower plants might be slow to reappear, although you can be sure that their seeds will be in the soil somewhere. If this is the case, you might like to hurry things along by deliberately introducing them into the turf. Have a look around your borders and the vegetable patch: you might be able to find some of these plants growing there (as weeds) and all you have to do then is transplant them into your lawn. There are also nurseries (including mail-order companies) that specialize in a variety of wild plants for just this sort of purpose. You can usually purchase them in 7cm (3in) pots, which is the ideal size for putting in the turf. This is a good way of obtaining primroses and cowslips, which are unlikely to reappear in a lawn. It's never worth scattering wildflower seed into a

Primroses are among the most desirable of spring flowers and they are generous with their blooms, too.

well-established lawn as most often the grasses and more vigorous wildings will discourage them from germinating. Be wary of planting anything that has to grow quite tall to flower, such as yarrow, otherwise you're into the realms of a wildflower meadow (see Don't Forget, opposite), which is quite a different kettle of fish.

If you're making a new lawn and sowing grass seed, your best bet is to plan in advance and incorporate some wildflower seed into the grass-seed mixture. Again, there are companies that will provide it ready mixed. Don't be too ambitious and don't expect miracles – it's often the case that wildflower seeds are less keen to germinate where they're wanted than where they're not, and the grass seed will tend to be much more vigorous to begin with. You can also purchase wildflower turf, but this usually contains plants that are more suitable for a wildflower meadow, so beware if all you want is a flowery lawn.

Care of a wildflower lawn

The most important thing to know about wildflowers is that they're not very fond of fertilizers, so stop feeding your lawn, or if you're starting from scratch never feed it. On the other side of the coin, grass likes food, so by ceasing feeding you're discouraging lush grass growth. This is beneficial for wildflowers, which find grass a bit of an overpowering bedfellow.

Secondly, you mustn't use weedkiller, for fairly obvious reasons.

If you find your lawn becoming overwhelmed with unwanted plants, the best thing to do is to spot-treat them, and don't let them seed.

Finally, there's mowing. You already know to allow the grass to grow a little longer between cuts, but you should also remove grass clippings from the surface. In a perfect world, you also need to be prepared to let the grass grow even longer than 5cm (2in) once in a while, because this allows the wildflowers to gain greater strength and in the case of cowslips and others that flower on longer stems, enables them to bloom and set seed. Find out when your particular favourites flower and have a lazy few weeks not mowing during this time.

The pale red-brown young leaves of the Japanese maple (*Acer palmatum* 'Burgundy Lace') frame a meadow of bluebells and dandelions.

Ground-cover plants

So-called ground-cover plants can perform a range of useful jobs in the garden. They're wonderful as an alternative to grass in small, shady or dry areas, especially if you want to fill spaces beside lawns or patios without making a more formal flower border. But ground-cover plants are probably most valued for their ability to spread over areas of hard surfacing, softening its impact but without intruding too much.

When you're making a patio, it's worth leaving out a couple or more paving slabs or bricks so that you can plant directly into the patio area itself. This has the double benefit of softening the hard lines of the surface while also lessening its stark newness. If you're lucky (or if you leave some of the joints between the pavers un-grouted), the plants will self-seed, creating an even more effortless informality. A great plant for this is Virginia stock (*Malcolmia maritima*). It has fragrant, four-petalled, pink, purple or white flowers on low-growing plants that can survive on minimal root runs. Simply scattering the seeds in late spring should ensure you get years of blooms.

Spreading ground cover
If you want to create a natural, spreading effect, choose low-growing, creeping or trailing plants. Thyme (*Thymus, see* right and opposite) and chamomile (*Chamaemelum, see* opposite) are suitable, as are aubretias, fleabane (*Erigeron karvinskianus, see* above) and gold dust (*Aurinia saxatilis*). Grow these in ribbon beds alongside paths, beside your patio or even by your doorstep.

Shady areas are always more of a challenge than sunny ones, but the smaller-leaved ivies will make a good job of filling an empty patch and you could always try mind-your-own-business (*Soleirolia soleirolii*). This plant's tiny little leaves belie its indomitable nature – don't turn your back on it, otherwise it may go where you don't want it to. In fact, this is the one drawback of ground-covering plants – they are a bit like nature, that is, they abhor a vacuum: if they come across space they will take up residence.

Upright ground cover
You might prefer to make the most of the crisp lines and sharp angles of your paving or decking and put the emphasis on formality with upright plants that tend to stay in a neat shape

Plants with a spreading habit encourage experimentation – or do it themselves. ① Fleabane (*Erigeron karvinskianus*) has made a work of art of these steps. ② A charming rustic bench with a chamomile cushion nestles in a carpet of lavender and thyme.

(or don't mind being trimmed into one). Box, lavender (*see* opposite) and small hebes are all excellent choices, and would also look good alongside a straight-edged lawn or gravelled area. Sempervivums provide interesting textures and don't mind the dryish conditions that might prevail on a south-facing patio, while in a cooler site the neat outline of hosta leaves would be thrown into relief by paving.

Herb lawns

If you like the idea of a lawn of some sort but would rather avoid grass, or if you'd like a different type of 'carpet' for a separate area of the garden, you might like to create a lawn made entirely from aromatic flowering herbs. Herb lawns are beautifully fragrant and can look wonderful, but unlike grass they don't stand much wear and are therefore suitable only for areas that don't get walked on much. There are only two real contenders for a herb lawn: thyme and chamomile.

Chamomile (*Chamaemelum nobile*) needs to be grown in free-draining, acid soil. It has soft, feathery, rich-green leaves, which smell a little like green apples when crushed, and white daisy flowers; the variety 'Treneague' (*see* above) doesn't flower. Sow seed in pots in early spring or buy small plants. Plant out the young plants in early summer – you need to space them about 15cm (6in) apart. Chamomile turf is also available – it is pricey but saves you a lot of bother – lay it as you would normal turf (*see* pages 43–4). While it's lovely to walk upon a fragrant mass of chamomile plants, it has to be admitted that they aren't nearly as tough as grass. Chamomile lawns look good in the first year and

A scented chamomile path made from *Chamaemelum nobile* 'Treneague' edged with *Lavandula angustifolia* 'Hidcote'.

need only occasional trimming, but they're short-lived and soon become ragged and holey, though you can replace individual plants as necessary.

Thyme (*Thymus serpyllum*) is low growing with a creeping habit, fragrant leaves and small, insect-attracting, purple-pink flowers. It likes poorish soil, sun and good drainage. Buy small plants in spring and plant out in early summer, spacing them about 20–22cm (8–9in) apart, closer for a more immediate effect, but be prepared for frequent trimming. Like many thymes, this can be short-lived in less-than-perfect conditions and it will also need an annual trim in late summer or early autumn, after which it may not look so pretty for a while. It won't stand up to much (if any) pedestrian traffic, so you should make a stepping-stone path through it – the plants will soon grow up around the stones and disguise them.

Ground-cover plants for small areas

Buttonweed (*Leptinella atrata*)
Forms carpets of evergreen foliage that are so dense that weeds are often smothered. It grows only 2.5cm (1in) high, so will never need trimming, and has creamy flowers in summer.

Corsican mint (*Mentha requienii*)
A ground-hugging mint with strongly scented leaves: it's a wonderful clear-the-head type aroma. It grows on moisture-retentive soil, preferably in a shady site, and slowly slides along the ground, almost like a large lichen. You'd be optimistic to try to fill a large space with it, but it's great close to paths and patios.

Creeping jenny
(*Lysimachia nummularia*)
This ground-covering plant, often sold for hanging baskets, sends out long stems that root and form new plants as they grow. It has rounded, bright-green leaves and yellow flowers and doesn't need clipping. If it likes its spot in the garden, you may never get rid of it – be warned. 'Aurea' has yellow-green leaves.

Kidney weed (*Dichondra micrantha*)
This is sold in garden centres for growing in hanging baskets and containers. It has silvery-green leaves that grow on long stems. It will tolerate light shade and heavy soils, and needs plenty of water.

Pennyroyal (*Mentha pulegium*)
A moth- and insect-repelling plant, pennyroyal is peppermint scented with rooting stems that benefit from a little trampling underfoot. It needs sun and soil that doesn't get over-dry. The flowers, which you'll need to shear off to keep the plant low growing, are popular with bees and butterflies.

Don't forget

Lawns that are made mostly of non-grass plants cannot be mown. Most herbs and ground-cover plants can be left to grow naturally or you have to cut them with shears for a neater effect. Weed control can be difficult because the weeds get established before you have time to notice. The most troublesome weed in these lawns is grass!

Plants for hard surfaces

Plants greatly enhance any area of hard surfacing, enlivening expanses of paving, brick or gravel. There are no hard-and-fast rules about what to plant beside your path, patio or deck, but you'll find the results more satisfactory if you choose plants that have a long season of interest, a neat habit and that don't grow too fast so you're not having to cut back frequently.

Planting around patios, decks and paths

One or several trees or shrubs at the perimeter of a patio, deck or path will add interest in the form of height, shape and colour, and will also provide welcome shade and shelter. Plants in such situations soften the hard lines of paving and make a link between man-made structures and the garden.

The same small trees and shrubs suggested for lawns (*see* pages 99–103) will do well here. Try to select some plants with fragrant flowers or aromatic foliage, so you can enjoy their scent while you sit or walk past. Choose at least one evergreen so that you have something to look at

and enjoy through the winter. It's best to avoid conifers unless it's one of the narrowly columnar types, because their foliage is so dense, but evergreens with a finer canopy, such as a strawberry tree (*Arbutus* × *andrachnoides, see* page 101), can be very effective. Climbers like roses and wisteria, trained up walls, fences or supports, are also attractive.

Over time, shrubs may start to infiltrate your carefully laid seating or walking area, in which case either prune them back, 'lift their skirts' or dig them out and start again. Lifting the skirts involves removing lower

Hebes and box are among the permanent plants around this brick patio. Both have an exemplary tidy habit and are evergreen.

branches to reveal the trunk-like stems underneath and is a very effective way of pruning some larger shrubs – older specimens of rhododendron and pieris have attractive gnarled or textured bark that can be a feature in its own right.

Hard surfaces seem to be a magnet to leaves and other plant debris, so be prepared to sweep up on a regular basis – the pleasure of having plants in close proximity is worth this easy work. Be careful about planting trees close to buildings. Although many very old buildings have survived years of being bear-hugged by vast magnolias, wisterias and Virginia creepers, nowadays insurance companies are very jumpy about such risk-taking. Also, make sure that any trees, shrubs, climbers or other plants near a patio and, especially, near decking will not cast day-long shade or you'll be troubled with dangerous slippery patches.

Adding containers

Patios and decking are among the most perfect places for growing plants in decorative containers. If you're well organized, you can plant up a series of pots with a variety of different plants so that you can have a continuous display of flowers and foliage all year. Alternatively, you can have just a few permanent pots for specimen plants that are pretty to look at all year round.

Don't forget

All plants need care and regular attention in a garden environment. If you don't have much time to spare, limit plant numbers and make sure the few you have really thrive.

A compact form of catmint is perfectly placed along either side of this gravel path. The aromatic leaves will release their fragrance as feet brush past.

Even out of flower, this wisteria makes an impact over a pergola and provides shade for lush foliage plants – and seated diners – beneath.

or small shrubs, you do need to start with the largest possible container and be prepared to pot up several times over the course of a few years. Choose a pot that is the size of your plant's rootball plus about 2.5–4cm (1–1½in) all round. Don't be tempted to put a plant in a container that's way too big for it, as this often means it will be overwatered and die as a result. With bigger pots and short-term plantings, save weight by filling the bottom third or so with polystyrene packaging, which will take up space but weighs virtually nothing. Long-term residents need as much potting compost as possible, so you'll have to resign yourself to having stationary pots, or moving them on a trolley if necessary. It's important

By limiting the choice of plants, materials and colours, the designer of this decked roof garden has created an oasis of calm and style.

An artful jumble of foliage and flowers produces a joyful picture in this raised bed surrounded by chimney-pot planters.

Picking pots

There are no limits to the type of pots to use for hard surfaces. If you're planting a succession of containers for display throughout the year it makes sense to choose some that are easy to move about. With decking it's particularly important to consider the weight of the filled container, as you should shift pots around from time to time to avoid the wood being stained or rotting under them. Using pot feet to assist drainage is very sensible on any hard surface.

For summer annuals, small pots will often be sufficient, but for longer-term planting, say of bamboo

Don't forget
Containers and raised beds are ideal for plants that won't thrive in your garden soil – perhaps because they need acid conditions (for example rhododendrons and camellias) or better drainage (Mediterranean plants and most alpines hate having wet feet). If you're keen on DIY you could make your own raised bed out of timber, dry-stone walling or bricks (*see* pages 79, 81 and 116).

that such pots won't get blown over by the wind, so make sure they aren't going to be top-heavy.

What to plant into

It's worth taking some care with potted plants, as they're part of your patio or decking decoration and on full view to all visitors. Plant them into good-quality loamless (also known as soilless) potting compost with some added water-retaining crystals – or choose a compost that already has water-retaining abilities (they've just added the crystals for you). The crystals absorb water and then slowly release it so your plants get a longer-lasting supply, but this doesn't mean you don't have to water regularly – at least daily during hot weather. Use some slow-release fertilizer too, to ensure that the plants never go hungry. Plants that are going to stay in place for longer than the summer months are best planted in a mix of loamless and loam-based potting compost, to give them something more 'meaty' to root into.

Tulips in pots herald the spring. As the flowers fade, the pots can be ushered out of sight to be replaced by early summer blooms.

A frame of permanent planting including ceanothus and topiary box is augmented by temporary colourful potted displays in this urban garden.

Cordylines and young Italian cypresses are very effective in this seating area. Their restrained habits mean they can be allowed to grow here for many years.

Plants for containers

When it comes to plants for pots, you can't go far wrong with annuals. They're generally easy to grow and produce prodigious amounts of flower from very early summer often into mid-autumn if the weather is kind. You can choose from a wide variety of sizes, habits and colours. The only drawback of annuals is that they do their thing in the summer months and leave you with nothing over winter and into spring. However, bulbs are excellent for

some early colour on the patio, and there are plenty of flowering bulbs for summer, too – lilies, agapanthus and dahlias all make good pot plants and give a fantastic display from midsummer into autumn, year after year, with very little in the way of attention. For the dark winter months, small-leaved variegated ivies, evergreen clematis (*C. armandii*) and evergreen shrubs, such as box (*Buxus sempervirens*) and small hebes, can be counted on to ensure your patio or deck looks loved.

Creating raised beds

Permanent raised beds are another option on patios and decks. They provide a greater volume of soil than containers and more space; as a result, plants grow more like they would in a garden border.

Depending on their size, raised beds can be filled in much the same way as containers or you can use topsoil mixed with garden compost, but put a layer of grit at the bottom to ensure good drainage. If you plant annuals into raised beds, be prepared to replace at least the top 15–20cm (6–8in) of the compost each year; with long-term residents, top-dressing with a soil and garden compost mix each year and adding slow-release fertilizer should be sufficient. (For information on constructing raised beds, *see* pages 79 and 81.)

A bold experiment in colour and planting pays off in this show garden. Cottage-garden plants grow happily in these raised beds, unperturbed by their bright surroundings.

Green roofs

If you're feeling adventurous, consider creating a green (living) roof on top of your house, outbuilding or even shed. Green roofs are the perfect way to extend the garden, making the most of every available inch of space, and they're hailed as helping the environment in many ways.

Green roofs are like a newfangled thatch – they're usually made from mats planted with masses of drought-resistant plants, particularly sedum, but on bigger roofs with plenty of space and soil depth, the sky's the limit – almost. Large-size green roofs are the sort of thing that enlightened commercial companies are starting to put on their buildings – the roofs are strong enough to walk on, and as long as the soil is 15cm (6in) or more deep they can include a wide variety of plants including shrubs and even small trees. The smaller, domestic versions, which are not designed for walking on and have shallower soil, also have a great number of benefits.

The advantages of green roofs
Green roofs are a huge bonus for wildlife – they attract butterflies, bees, beetles and worms, which in turn provide food for birds. Of benefit to humans is that they're attractive and provide an additional layer of insulation in winter. Also, because vegetation deflects rather than absorbs ultra-violet rays, they keep living areas nice and cool in summer. In heavy rain, the plants on the roof absorb water and release it slowly without putting a great strain on the house drainage system, which can result in flooding.

Simply dripping with growth, this shed has the ultimate green roof. It is easy to imagine the tremendous weight of these abundant succulents.

Installing a green roof and aftercare
Mats for green roofs are available from a number of suppliers and many of these will install them too, which may be a good idea as you can't simply throw a sedum mat over any building. Although a shallow-pitched roof is acceptable, any angle greater than 15 degrees may mean that the plants at the top of the slope suffer from being too dry and you'll need to provide irrigation. The roof must be completely waterproofed, which for a shed or small structure is usually done with a membrane of rubber, PVC or polythene, although on larger structures concrete can be used. The structure may also need to be strengthened, as a green roof can be very heavy, particularly when wet.

Once the sedum mat is in place it pretty much takes care of itself, but you'll need to check it once in a while for unwanted seedlings, which may start to take root. The sedum plants are low growing with fleshy leaves and they can survive where there is very little soil, but they do need about four hours of sun a day in order to flourish. In summer they produce small flowers in soft shades of yellow, pink or white and it is these that attract the insects.

Aftercare

The most important thing you can do with your patio, lawn and any other part of your garden is to enjoy them. It's so easy to get carried away with the minutiae of tending to your plot that you don't ever take the time to sit back and think – 'I did this'. That said, to be able to continue to enjoy them, you'll need to take care of them, which means being organized. This short section is intended to help you in this department. There's nothing like time for slipping through your fingers and, if you find this happens to you, these seasonal lists of jobs that need doing might come in useful.

Lawns season by season

Lawns need far more work on a much more regular basis than an area of hard surfacing such as a patio or deck (*see* page 123). However, if you keep your lawn in good health, the work isn't all that time-consuming: it takes much longer to weed a flower border than it does to mow the same amount of lawn, for example, and the results are more immediately apparent. Once you get into the habit of looking after a lawn, it all becomes second nature, too. You might even find mowing relaxing, and seeing the results of your labour is certainly satisfying.

Climatic variation

Our islands are renowned for their weather and though Britain is small, we experience great variation in climate from one end to the other and across the country too. Spring comes to southern England perhaps three weeks earlier than it does to northern Scotland, so garden jobs such as sowing seed or mowing the lawn will invariably start earlier in the year. The seasons given here are a rough guideline, so you may need to make adjustments to timing according to where you live.

Early spring

You could start mowing now (*see* page 53), but only if conditions are mild and the grass has started to grow. Leave it until a bit later in cold regions or if the ground is very wet. The lawn might take as many as two cuts this season, but don't overdo it – simply snip off the very tops of the grass blades. Treat mossy areas with moss killer.

Another job for this time of year is to tidy the lawn edges (*see* pages 45–6). It's a very satisfying cosmetic job with great rewards and it can be carried out over a few fine days. The sooner you get it done, the better the lawn will look, even if you do nothing else to it at this stage.

Other optional tasks
- Treat individual lawn weeds by easing out their rosettes with a daisy grubber or old kitchen knife.
- Rake the lawn gently to get rid of leaves and other debris.
- Roll the lawn with a cylinder mower that has the blades out of cutting reach. Do this during a dry spell as otherwise you risk compacting the soil rather than simply smoothing out any small lumps and bumps.

Mid-spring

Mowing starts to be more frequent in mid-spring, depending on where you live. Keep the lawn at about 2.5cm (1in) or slightly longer if the weather is dry; fine lawns can be shorter, at 1.5cm (½in) or so. Check that the lawn is looking healthy, and dig out any areas of coarse grass and individual weeds. Fill the resulting holes with soil and re-seed or re-turf (*see* page 65).

Now is the best time to seed any new areas, or wait until late summer or early autumn. The same goes for turf, which otherwise should be done in mid-autumn. Water areas of new turf regularly to ensure the grass's survival.

Other optional tasks
- Proprietary weed-and-feed products (*see* pages 60–1) can be used towards the end of mid-spring, but late spring is often more suitable. If you use lawn sand (*see* page 61) remember to rake out the dead moss a couple of weeks later (*see* page 57).

> Early in the year, do several tip-skimming cuts rather than one drastic restyle.

Late spring

Mowing becomes a weekly duty at some point in late spring. Sudden flushes of grass growth can take you by surprise, so be ready to get out there mid-week if necessary. If you didn't do it in mid-spring, feed your lawn now and water it in well. With a combined weed-and-feed product you need the grass to be dry but the soil to be moist. Don't apply it on a windy day, and water if no rain falls within two days or so.

Other optional tasks
- In dry weather, water a new lawn well (*see* pages 51–2) so long as there is no hosepipe ban. Let established lawns find their own water. It is unlikely to remain dry for long at this time of year and they will quickly revive in the first shower.

Early summer

Mowing may become a twice-weekly job now – again, the ideal height when the weather is not too dry is 2.5cm (1in) or 1.5cm (½in) on fine lawns. Trim the lawn edges often to prevent the grass growing into your borders (*see* pages 45–6).

Spot-treat any persistent weeds (*see* page 61) or dig them out, and rake around patches of clover before mowing – this way, the mowing does maximum damage to its running stems. Feed the lawn if it is looking pale or the grass growth is weak: a high-nitrogen liquid feed is most suitable at this time of year, being faster acting than granules.

Other optional tasks
■ New lawns may need watering, but cutting with the blades slightly higher so that the grass is 3cm (1¼in) long, or 2cm (¾in) for fine lawns, will preserve water in the soil and reduce the need for watering.

Midsummer

Lawn duties in midsummer are much the same as they are in early summer. If you're going on holiday at any time in summer, do a cut before going and remember to make two or three increasingly short cuts when you return rather than one drastic cut (*see* page 53). If you're away for more than two weeks, get someone to come in and do a mow or two for you, to avoid your hard work being for naught.

Late summer

Continue as for early and midsummer. This is the last season that you can use high-nitrogen feeds and pretty much the last season when weedkilling with chemicals will be effective.

Other optional tasks
■ Sowing seed can be done towards the end of summer (*see* pages 40–2), but early autumn is usually better from a weather point of view.

Perk up flagging lawns with a high-nitrogen liquid feed. By delivering it diluted in water you ensure it gets straight to where it's needed and quickly.

Early autumn

Like mid-spring, early autumn is a busy time in the garden. The lawn-maintenance routine starts now: scarify, aerate, top-dress, in that order (*see* pages 57–9). Use an autumn feed if necessary (*see* page 49) and carry out repairs, such as removal of bumps and hollows or re-seeding bare patches in the lawn (*see* page 65).

Worm casts will need brushing away before mowing – for autumn mowing, raise the blades by 5mm (¼in) to 3cm (1¼in) and 2cm (¾in) for fine lawns if you haven't already done so due to dry weather.

Other optional tasks
- Sow new lawns (*see* pages 40–2).

Don't forget

Autumn is the best time to be kind to your lawn. Set aside just one weekend to do all those routine jobs and the following year you'll be very glad you did.

Mid-autumn

Mowing becomes less frequent as the grass growth slows down with the colder weather. Don't be tempted to mow wet grass – brush off dew if you're really keen, or wait for a drier day. Trim lawn edges to keep a neat appearance over winter (*see* pages 45–6). Make the effort two or three times this season to sweep or rake leaves off the lawn (or mow them off if you think your mower will cope), otherwise they'll tend to congregate in a few areas where the wind blows them and the grass underneath will really suffer.

It's not too late to do lawn maintenance and repairs if you didn't do them in early autumn. Focus on wet or boggy areas – they will benefit particularly from aeration and top-dressing.

Other optional tasks
- Re-turf from now until late winter (*see* pages 43–4).

Late autumn

Lawn care needs to continue in pretty much the same way as it did in mid-autumn. During wet weather, don't walk on the lawn. If there's no avoiding it, use planks to make a makeshift path.

Sweep worm casts on the surface of the lawn with a besom broom. The fine bristles help to scatter the soil between the blades of grass.

Early winter

This is not a good time for any lawn, since the cold, wet weather tends to encourage any grass growth to be uneven and it can be difficult to find a suitable day for mowing. On fine days, continue raking leaves and neaten any edges that might benefit (*see* pages 45–6). Otherwise, make the most of the down time – spring is just around the corner!

Make use of a fine, dry winter's day to check over and clean your tools – that way, they'll be ready for use when they're needed in spring.

Midwinter

One of the secrets of a good lawn is to be prepared. While it's cold and wet outside, get the lawn mower serviced, if necessary. If you wait until early spring, when you start to need it, the people at your local lawn mower servicing shop will be up to their eyeballs in work and it might take them a month or so to get around to yours, by which time you'll be out there cutting the grass with a scythe! On an uneventful weekend, get out the other lawn maintenance tools and give them an overhaul – sharpen blades, clean tines, oil moving parts, check handles and generally make sure they're all working.

Don't walk on the lawn during frosty or very wet weather.

Other optional tasks
▪ If necessary, turfing can be done in fine weather (*see* pages 43–4).

Late winter

This is a lazy time for lawn lovers. Again, don't walk on the grass if it's frosty or wet, and if you need to in order to enjoy the snowdrops, make a note to put in a path or move the bulbs before next year. If the weather's mild, you might want to sweep away worm casts towards the end of the month (*see* page 62), but don't be tempted to mow.

Other optional tasks
▪ Prepare areas for sowing grass seed, which you do in early to mid-spring.
▪ Any turfing should be completed by the end of this season.

Maintaining hard surfaces

The amount of time you spend throughout the year caring for your garden's hard surfaces – whether it's a path, patio or deck – depends on the material they're made from and their position in the garden. For example, a deck needs more attention than a concrete patio, and a path that is situated under trees will need more attention than one that receives full sun all day. Deal with all unwanted weeds before they set seed.

An old kitchen knife is the ideal tool for winkling weeds from between pavers, although you'd be lucky to get the whole dandelion root out.

Paved patios and paths

Natural stone, concrete paving slabs and bricks weather with time and in most cases this improves their appearance. Concrete paving may develop a white bloom, which is caused by leaching out of the lime used in its manufacture. This bloom will disappear over time (but it may take a couple of years) and is nothing to worry about. You can clean it off, but it will tend to reappear until all the lime that can leach out has done so.

As far as maintenance goes, a quick brush every so often should be sufficient; use water and a stiff-bristled brush on light stains and dirt. If you want to do a spring clean, you can buy various cleaners to get rid of algae, oil stains and so on, but a pressure washer on a low setting will see off most problems. Don't overdo it though, as the force of the water can spoil surface textures and may damage the mortar in the joints.

Gravel and bark surfaces

Loose materials such as gravel and bark chippings can shift and sink into the soil so need topping up from time to time. Bark will rot eventually, so needs replacing within a few years. Watch out for weeds growing up through the gravel or bark.

Decking

All wood has a limited shelf life, even when pressure-treated, and constant exposure to the elements will take its toll, so you need to take good care of your deck. To prevent any areas becoming unduly damp, sweep regularly to remove plant and other debris. Once a year you need to undertake a lengthier programme of cleaning and preserving. Spring is a good time to do this.

There are several proprietary cleaners for decking; most are applied as a liquid. Follow the instructions given on the packet, which generally involve wetting the deck with water and sweeping the diluted cleaner over the surface, ensuring it goes into all the nooks and crannies. Some areas may need a second application, after which you hose the whole lot off.

Allow the deck to dry thoroughly (this may take a couple of days) before painting it with a wood preservative. It may be necessary to apply two coats.

Don't forget

Even neglected decks can be restored to something of their former glory through the judicious use of a cleaner followed by a couple of coats of preserving oil. If you inherit a deck and are not sure of its past history, clean and preserve as a precaution – it won't do any harm. With badly discoloured decks, consider using a stripper cleaner, but take great care of surrounding plants and structures and only ever apply it wearing protective gloves.

Index

Acknowledgements

BBC and Outhouse would like to thank the following for their assistance in preparing this book: Andrew McIndoe for his advice and guidance; Robin Whitecross for picture research; Lindsey Brown for proofreading; June Wilkins for the index.

Picture credits

Key t = top; b = bottom; l = left; r = right; c = centre

All photographs by Jonathan Buckley except the following:

GAP Photos Matt Anker 108br; Mark Bolton 100t; Elke Borkowski 14tl, 75t, 78b, 81t, 112, 113b; Leigh Clapp 98; Paul DeBois 99b; Carol Drake 101t; Ron Evans 88bl, 110(2); Fhf Greenmedia 75b; Tim Gainey 109; Suzie Gibbons 76l, 79t, 115b; John Glover 89b; Jerry Harpur 70(2), 86, 95, 114t, 115t, 116t, 116b, 117; Michael Howes 79b; Fiona Lea 100b; Zara Napier 42, 99t, 106t; Clive Nichols 81b, 92t, 102t; Brian North 85; Howard Rice 88br; J S Sira 4–5, 114b; Juliette Wade 83; Rob Whitworth 87b, 90tl, 101(4)

Garden World Images S. Keeble 47(3)

Andrew McIndoe 30, 31b, 33tr, 41br, 50, 60t, 60b, 61t, 61b

Clive Nichols 9b, 12t, 13t, 17t, 66, 67b, 68t, 70(1), 78t, 87t, 88t, 91, 92b, 93t, 93b, 94, 97, 101(3), 103t

Photolibrary Tips Italia/Zatac 65, Mark Winward 41bl

Thanks are also due to the following designers and owners whose gardens appear in the book:

Rosemary Alexander, Stoneacre 67t; Julian & Isabel Bannerman 70(2); Christopher Bradley-Hole 47(1); Gill Brown 24t; Fiona Bruce 9t; Declan Buckley 20; Beth Chatto, Beth Chatto Gardens 89t; Lady Collum, Clinton Lodge 111; Katherine Crouch 82(1); Data Nature Associates 66; Roy Day & Steve Hickling 90tr; Roja Dove 116t; Sam France 115t; Adam Frost 79b; Diarmuid Gavin 16, 17; Luciano Giubbilei 114t; Judith Glover 89b; Anthony Goff 31t; Bunny Guinness 68b; Diana Guy 105t; David Harber Sundials 87t; Trudi Harrison 41; Alison Hoghton & David Chase 22t, 76r; Kevin Hughes 12br; Paul Kelly 24t; Carol Klein 114b; Dominique Lafourcade 13t, 70(1); Rani Lall 11t, 21; Mark Laurence 88t, 97; Sarah Layton 94; Little Court 9b; Christopher Lloyd, Great Dixter 12bl, 105b, 106b, 110(1), 118; John Massey, Ashwood Nurseries 90b, 103b, 122t; Clare Matthews 93b; Michael Miller 82(3); A. Noel 78t; Christina Oates 15t, 80, 91; Philip Osman 68t; RHS Wisley 102t; Charlotte Rowe 67b, 93t; Ruth Salisbury 69l; Heather Scott 79t; Gill Siddell 39, 51; Vladmir Sitta 86; Carol & Malcolm Skinner, Eastgrove Cottage Garden Nursery 45b; Penny Smith 69r; Sue & Wol Staines, Glen Chantry 26, 121t; June Streets 11b; Mrs Stuart-Smith, Serge Hill 113t; Joe Swift & Sam Joyce for The Plant Room 15b, 82(2), 84, 120t; Kathy Taylor 17t, 81b, 92b; Tilgates Garden, Surrey 101(3); Alan Titchmarsh 87b, 102b; Sue Townsend 83; Oehme Van Sweden 95; Carole Vincent 82(4); Sue Ward, Ladywood 22b; Claire Whitehouse 75b, 116b; Wilkins Pleck 12t; Gay Wilson 8, 10t, 14r; Woodpeckers 103t; Wynniatt-Husey Clarke 92t; Helen Yemm, Eldenhurst 13b, 19